The Mystery Shopper's MANUAL

fifth edition

The Mystery Shopper's MANUAL

How to get paid to shop in your favorite stores, eat in your favorite restaurants, and more!

Cathy Stucker

The Mystery Shopper's Manual:

How to get paid to shop in your favorite stores, eat in your favorite restaurants, and more!

Published by:
Special Interests Publishing
4646 Hwy 6, #123
Sugar Land, TX 77478

Orders: 1-888-BOOK-888 (888-266-5888)

Royalty-free articles on mystery shopping, publishing, small business marketing and other topics are available to webmasters, and newsletter and ezine publishers at http://www.idealady.com/content.htm.

For more information on mystery shopping, visit Cathy Stucker on the web at http://www.IdeaLady.com/.

Cover design © 2002 TLC Graphics
http://www.TLCGraphics.com/

Interior illustrations © New Vision Technologies, Inc.

Printed in the United States of America

ISBN 1-888983-24-8

*This book is dedicated to
my husband, Michael Stucker,
in gratitude for your love and support,
even when you think I'm a little crazy!*

Acknowledgments

Many people generously shared their knowledge during the research and writing of this book. Information and time were contributed by Mike Bare and Greg Dale of Bare Associates International, Cheryl Durbin of Palm Scheduling Services, Mike Green of Green & Associates, Lorri Kern of Kern Scheduling Services, Mark Michelson of Michelson & Associates, Chuck Paul of A Closer Look, Sondra Pulford of Texas Shoppers Network, Charles Tinsley of The Shadow Agency, Brad Worthley of Brad Worthley International/BradWorthley.com, and others. Special thanks go to each of them for helping to make this book informative, realistic and useful to mystery shoppers.

Many mystery shoppers, as well as employees who have been mystery shopped, shared their experiences with me. Thank you to all of you.

Thanks to Tamara Dever and Erin Stark of TLC Graphics for the great cover design. And to all of my friends and colleagues who provided input and feedback on the book.

Preface

You can have fun and make extra money while providing an important service as a mystery shopper. This book shows you how. Its purpose is to help you understand the mystery shopping business so you can jump start your career as a professional mystery shopper. The information you'll find here comes right from the source: mystery shoppers, mystery shopping companies and schedulers.

Mystery shopping isn't a get-rich-quick scheme, and it's not money for nothing. It is an enjoyable way to make money, usually part time or in your spare time, by providing valuable customer service feedback to businesses.

The Mystery Shopper's Manual is the book I wish I had when I was getting started as a mystery shopper back in 1995. My goal in creating this book was to provide an honest look at mystery shopping and step-by-step instructions that you can use to get started.

I hope you will use *The Mystery Shopper's Manual* to become a successful professional shopper. For updates and more information about mystery shopping, please visit www.IdeaLady.com.

Cathy Stucker
March, 2002

Disclaimer:
Please Read

This book is designed to provide helpful and informative material about the mystery shopping business. The publisher and author are not engaged in rendering professional legal, accounting or other services in this book. If the reader requires personal assistance or advice, a qualified professional should be consulted.

Mystery shopping is not a get-rich-quick scheme. The amount of income earned by a mystery shopper depends on many factors, including the shopper's geographic location, prior experience, availability to work, and ability and willingness to perform to required standards. Most mystery shoppers should not expect to rely on mystery shopping to generate all of their income. The author and publisher make no guarantees regarding the number of mystery shopping assignments a shopper may receive or the income to be derived.

Every effort has been made to make the information herein as accurate and complete as possible. However, there may be typographical or other mistakes. Information which was correct at the time of publication may become inaccurate with the passage of time as the industry evolves.

The author and publisher shall have no liability or responsibility to any person or entity with respect to any loss or damage caused, or alleged to be caused, directly or indirectly, by use or misuse of the information in this book.

Table of Contents

What is Mystery Shopping?

Mystery shoppers visit businesses "disguised as normal customers," and do the things other customers do—ask questions, make a purchase, make a return—but with a twist. These undercover customers are trained to evaluate the businesses and their employees. After a visit, the mystery shopper completes a report or questionnaire detailing what occurred during the visit.

Mystery shopping goes by many names, including secret shopping, service evaluation, service check and others. No matter what it's called, mystery shopping is an important tool for businesses that care about how they are perceived by customers.

Why Do Businesses Hire Mystery Shoppers?

Mystery shops have different objectives. In general, shops are done to find out about the level of service provided to customers. However, mystery shoppers may also be asked to verify that cashiers are properly handling cash, the business is clean and merchandise is displayed neatly, staff persons are knowledgeable, etc. As a mystery shopper, you may be asked to verify if employees used a certain phrase (such as, "Thank you for shopping at Mega Mart.") or if they used suggestive selling techniques ("Would you like fries with that?").

You may be asked to shop a clients' competitors, so the client can compare their operation to others. Mystery shoppers may monitor pricing, or verify that businesses are in compliance with professional standards or government regulations.

One common misconception about mystery shoppers is that they are just looking for what is wrong. In fact, a mystery shopper is there to provide an objective view of the business, and they report on the good as well as the not-so-good.

Mystery shoppers seek the answers to questions. Were you greeted when you entered the store? Were the shelves properly stocked? Was the store clean? Did the rest rooms have soap and tissue? Was the salad bar completely stocked with fresh vegetables? How long did it take to be served? Did the salesperson tell you about the available service contract? Did the cashier properly count out your change? After they leave the business, they fill out a form or write a report describing what they observed.

When evaluating businesses, mystery shoppers are the eyes and ears of the business owner. Shoppers tell them how customers see the business. Most businesses have service standards and rules for safety and security. As a mystery shopper, you tell the business owner whether his employees are living up to the standards and following the rules.

How Is the Information Used?

Businesses use the information from shopper reports to reward good employees, identify training deficiencies, make stores safer for employees and customers, and much more. Companies may base performance evaluations and bonus pay outs at least in part on the results of mystery shopping.

The data obtained through mystery shops allow businesses to monitor the performance of one location when compared to another, or how the performance of the same location has improved over time.

Mystery shopping is also valuable for the *sentinel effect*. When employees know that they will be mystery shopped—but they don't know when or by whom—they will give every customer excellent service. This is especially true when the results of mystery shops are used in employee performance evaluations.

The Need for Mystery Shopping

Today's business environment is extremely competitive. Companies that fail to provide excellent service will not survive. Studies show that a satisfied customer will tell three other people about his experience. A dissatisfied customer will tell ten to twelve people. All too often, though, the customer won't tell the business owner or manager.

Not only do companies face loss of business from poor service, the actions of their employees may cause them to be sued by customers or fined by the government. With so much at stake, mystery shoppers provide a valuable service by identifying potential problems which the business owner can correct before they result in a major liability.

Who Are the Mystery Shoppers?

Because mystery shoppers look like typical customers (and are, in most ways, typical customers) almost anyone can become a mystery shopper. Shoppers may be any (adult) age, male or female. They may be employed, self-employed, unemployed, retired or full time homemakers.

What makes mystery shoppers different from other customers is that they want to help improve customer service and make some extra money while doing so, and they are specially trained to evaluate businesses and report their findings.

Most shoppers get into this business because it is fun. They love to get the perks, such as "free" food and merchandise, and even make a little money while they're getting this free stuff! Although mystery shopping can be fun, it is a business and you will have important responsibilities as a mystery shopper.

If you are interested in working flexible, part time hours, and getting paid to shop, eat and more while providing an important service to businesses, this book can help you. Read on to get the inside story on mystery shopping.

What Do
Mystery Shoppers Do?

Now that you know what mystery shopping is and why businesses are mystery shopped, let's go along on a shop to find out what mystery shoppers actually do.

Janice Rogers is watching, taking stock of everything around her, as she pulls into the parking lot. Loose carts, trash, potholes—nothing escapes her attention. As she enters the store, she notices that a greeter is there, saying hello and offering her a cart. She walks through the store to the camera department. She asks a salesperson, Steve, if he has any fully-automatic 35mm cameras. He points in the direction of a display case and says, "Over there," but does not escort her to the case or offer to show any cameras. Janice asks if he can show her which models have zoom lenses. Steve responds to her question and takes several minutes to point out features on the cameras she asks about.

After her encounter with Steve, Janice stops in the rest room. It's clean, but there is no soap in the dispensers. Then, Janice selects a product to purchase and heads for the checkouts. Anna, the cashier, greets Janice with "Good afternoon," and a smile. She rings up Janice's purchase quickly and correctly. Janice pays with a credit card, and as she hands Janice her purchase, Anna says, "Thank you for shopping with us, Mrs. Rogers."

Back in her car, Janice records the whole experience on a report form. From the poor appearance of the parking lot to the excellent service of the cashier, all will be noted.

What just happened here? Janice is a mystery shopper. Her job is to see how well the employees at stores, restaurants, gas stations, banks, and other businesses do their jobs. She will write a report about her shopping trip, including the good and the bad, that will go to store management. In return, she will be paid a fee, plus an allowance for the purchase she made at the store.

This is just one example of how mystery shoppers work. If you have never heard of mystery shopping before, you may be surprised to learn that there are thousands of people who get paid to shop at their favorite stores, then record their observations on a simple report form. Even if you are familiar with the concept of mystery shopping, you may be amazed at the types of businesses that use mystery shoppers, and the opportunities that exist for you.

Who Uses
Mystery Shoppers?

You may think of restaurants or department stores when you think of mystery shopping, but almost any business that deals with the public has a need for mystery shoppers.

Examples of businesses currently using mystery shoppers include:

amusement parks
apartment complexes
automobile dealers
auto repair shops
banks
bars and clubs
boutiques
brokerage houses
car rental agencies
casinos
convenience stores
copy and print shops
credit card issuers
credit unions
day care centers

department stores
discount stores
dry cleaners
fast food chains
financial services
gas stations
grocery stores
hair salons
health care providers
health clubs
home builders
hospitals
hotels and resorts
insurance companies
marinas

movie theaters
museums
nursing homes
outlet malls
pet shops and groomers
restaurants
RV parks

self-storage facilities
shoe stores
specialty retail stores
tourist attractions
truck and trailer rental
video rental stores
vision care providers

Mystery shoppers are also used by the government to check up on the businesses it regulates. For example, the Federal Deposit Insurance Corporation (FDIC) hired a firm to review how banks sell mutual funds. The government received many complaints from consumers who said they were mislead or given incorrect information by bank employees. The project included sending mystery shoppers to between 3,000 and 4,000 banks nationwide. Each shopper received a list of questions to ask to make sure banks are adequately explaining to customers that the mutual funds and annuities they sell are not insured by the federal government.

The Department of Housing and Urban Development has used mystery shopping to identify discrimination in housing and lending, and the Comptroller of the Currency uses shoppers to review banks' lending practices.

Government agencies at all levels also use mystery shopping to evaluate the service they provide to their citizen customers. That means that you might have the opportunity to mystery shop your local department of motor vehicles office or neighborhood post office.

Do You Have What it Takes to Be a Mystery Shopper?

When mystery shopping companies were asked what makes someone a good mystery shopper, they came up with remarkably similar answers. Several said that their best mystery shoppers are those who care about customer service and want to help businesses improve. Although they like making extra money and getting the free perks that come with mystery shopping, the best mystery shoppers truly enjoy the work and aren't in it just for the money.

According to the companies surveyed, a mystery shopper must be:

Reliable
This is a business, and companies depend on you to complete your shop as assigned. The biggest complaint of mystery shopping companies is that shoppers take assignments, don't do them and don't communicate with the company. Fulfill this basic expectation and you will be off to a good start.

Organized
You may have to juggle multiple assignments with different requirements and deadlines from more than one company.

Observant
During a shop you will have to get names, descriptions, and other details.

Objective
Mystery shopping is not opinion research, and you are not writing a review. Most questions on a mystery shopping report form are yes/no. Either something happened or it didn't. Something was true or it was not. State the facts.

Flexible
A shop may have to be done within a short time frame, or the client may require that it be done at a certain time or on a certain day. The more flexible you are about when you can shop, the more valuable you are to the mystery shopping company.

Honest
Don't try to fake a report or answers on the report. First of all, you should have the integrity to do the job right. If that's not enough motivation for you, you should know that you will probably be caught. There are ways to verify the information in your report, so don't make it up.

Thorough
Carefully prepare for the shop and know exactly what is expected of you. When doing the shop, do everything you were instructed to do and get all of the required information. Completely answer all questions on the form, including appropriate comments and narratives. Check your report for accuracy and completeness before submitting it.

A Good Writer
The comments and narratives you write should make the reader feel as if they are there, seeing what you saw. You don't need to be a brilliant writer, but you must be able to paint a vivid picture in words.

What Education and Experience Does a Mystery Shopper Need?

Some companies prefer that you have previous experience in mystery shopping or consumer research, but most companies don't care whether or not you are experienced. One company said that an advantage of using inexperienced shoppers is that they don't have any bad habits that have to be trained out of them!

Companies may give preference to shoppers with experience in the industries they shop. So, if you have worked in retail, hospitality, or other service fields, that gives you an edge.

Most companies don't have specific educational requirements. Better-educated shoppers may have stronger writing skills, but the writing skills are more important than how you got them.

What Equipment Does a Shopper Need?

More and more, mystery shopping companies are relying on the Internet to recruit and train shoppers, make assignments, and receive reports. While at the time of this writing it is still possible to get some mystery shopping jobs without a computer or Internet access, it is getting harder all the time.

Most of the large mystery shopping companies will expect you to have access to a computer and the Internet, including email. This is because it makes it easier for them to assign shops and process reports. Also, many of their clients are demanding faster access to report data, and the Internet facilitates much faster access than mailing paper copies of reports.

If you don't have a computer at home, you may be able to use one at work (make sure it's not against company policy) or at your local library. But consider getting a computer and Internet account at home. The cost has come down significantly over the last few years, and because you will use it for business some or all of the cost may be tax deductible.

Some companies' reports are Microsoft Word or Excel documents. If you have those programs, and know how to use them, it is a plus. (Although it is not a requirement at most companies.)

Depending on where you live and the nature of the assignments, some companies will want you to have a driver's license and a car. They may also ask for proof that you have auto insurance.

Once you get beyond these basic requirements, there aren't a lot of hard and fast rules. Every company has different procedures and requirements, but here are some of the items mentioned as "good to have." That means that they generally aren't required, but it may be a plus if you have them.

Answering machine, voice mail, mobile phone or pager

If a company needs to reach you (with a question about a report or to make a last-minute assignment) they need to reach you quickly. They don't want to call a number where there is no answer or get a busy signal because you are online. Remember to check messages frequently and return calls promptly.

Fax

This is good to have to submit receipts and other paperwork. If you don't have a fax, receipts may be scanned and emailed or sent via postal mail.

Scanner

Receipts may be faxed, mailed or scanned and emailed. A scanner offers you a way submit receipts and other paperwork via email.

Stopwatch (or digital watch with stopwatch)

You may need to time transactions. Remember when timing to be discreet.

Micro-cassette recorder

You may be asked to make an audio tape of the shop, or you may choose to audio tape as a way of capturing the information you need to write the report. Again, remember to be discreet.

Camera

Generally not used for mystery shopping, it may be a plus or even a requirement for some merchandising assignments.

Digital camera

As with a standard camera, a digital camera is generally not used for mystery shopping, but may be helpful or even a requirement for some merchandising assignments.

The mystery shopping company's application will ask whether you have any of these items that are important to them. If they don't ask, you may volunteer the information in your resume or in a comments section of the application.

Can You Make Money Doing This?

Yes, you can really get paid to shop. Mystery shopping isn't a get-rich-quick scheme, and it's not money for nothing. But mystery shopping can be easy and fun, and it is a great way to make extra money in your spare time while doing things you have to do anyway. You've got to shop and eat, right?

Most assignments can be completed within a range of days and times, so you have flexibility about when you work. You will usually be offered assignments close to your home, or in areas you have indicated you are willing to travel to, so you can do the shops while you are running other errands. Many of the shops I do are in stores and restaurants I go to regularly, so I'd be there anyway. This way, I'm getting paid to be there.

How much money you make will depend on how many shops you do and how much you are paid for each shop. When you work as a contract mystery shopper, you can't count on a certain income from month to month.

While some companies may keep you busy, in many cases you will receive only one or two jobs in a month. By contracting with many companies, the number of shops you do and the income you receive could increase.

Pay for mystery shops varies, depending on how much time is required, if any special expertise is needed, and if you receive a reimbursement for goods or services. You may receive a bonus if you accept a hard-to-fill assignment, or a rush job.

Pay Structure

Pay for a mystery shop may be:

Reimbursement only, where you are paid for a required purchase. For example, you may do a restaurant shop where your meal costs for two people are reimbursed with no additional fee paid.

Fee only, where you receive a set fee for completing the shop but there is no purchase reimbursement. This is common for shops where there is no purchase requirement, such as banks and apartment complexes.

Fee plus reimbursement, where you receive both a fee and reimbursement for a required purchase. You may find this when doing retail or restaurant shops, as well as others involving a required purchase.

When you are reimbursed for a required purchase, the purchase allowance may be used for anything you wish, or you may be told to purchase a specific item. If the required purchase is merchandise (not a service) you may have the option of keeping the item or returning it and keeping the cash.

Although it's not typical, you may be paid a mileage allowance for some shops. Usually, companies will schedule you for shops near your home or other places you've indicated that you are willing to go. However, there are times when it is hard to locate a shopper in the area. If you are asked to do one of these shops and make a special trip out of your usual area, you may be offered a bonus or mileage allowance.

Most companies do not pay expenses such as postage or fax fees to submit a receipt. They consider this minimal expense part of your fee, and don't make a separate reimbursement. Many companies have toll-free fax lines or allow you to scan and email receipts to them, so you would not have to incur any expense.

Fees and Reimbursements

There is no such thing as a "typical" mystery shopping fee. The requirements for each shop are different, and so are each company's policies. *The fee ranges mentioned here are for illustration purposes only. Shops offered to you may pay more or less than the amounts suggested.*

Many times when you are reimbursed for a purchase that has value, you will receive only a small additional fee or no fee at all. For example, if you receive free meals, a hair cut, a vision examination, or other benefit, you fee may be small or nonexistent.

You will be told what fee you will receive, and what the available reimbursement is when the shop is offered to you. You decide if it is worthwhile and if you want to do it. If a significant portion of the compensation is reimbursement based, and the required purchase is not of value to you, you might not want to do the shop.

As an example, your compensation for shopping a vision care provider might be a free eye exam, a discount on glasses or contact lenses, and a fee such as $10 or $20. If you don't need a vision examination or new glasses, it might not be worthwhile for you to do the shop just for the fee. On the other hand, if you are due for an eye exam, the value you receive could make this very attractive to you.

If a purchase is required, you will pay for it out of pocket, and receive your reimbursement when you are paid for the shop. It can take a few days to several weeks to get paid, with three to five weeks being typical. Using a credit card to pay (if allowed) gives you more time before you have to come up with the cash. Many times, you will have your reimbursement from the mystery shopping company before you have to pay your credit card bill. Occasionally, you will receive gift certificates or vouchers to pay for some or all of your purchase, so you won't have to pay then wait for reimbursement.

Restaurant reimbursements may range from $8 or $10 for a fast food shop to $150, $200 or more for a fine dining shop. Many buffet or full service restaurants will reimburse $20 to $50. The reimbursement level is based on the cost of meals at that restaurant, and will usually cover reasonable costs for two people. You won't be paid more than you spend, so if the maximum reimbursement is $40 and you spend $38, you'll get $38. The instructions will tell you if there are specific items you should or should not order, such as alcohol. Your reimbursement includes the tip in a full service restaurant or fine dining establishment.

Bar shops often reimburse a purchase of $20 to $50, and your purchase may include a snack or meal as well as one or two alcoholic beverages for the shopper and a companion.

Many retail shops don't include a purchase reimbursement. You may be asked to make a return of the item purchased and report on the return transaction. Some retail shops include a token reimbursement, such as $2 to $5, so you can make a small purchase. However, others will include greater reimbursement or a significant discount on your purchase. For example, you might receive 50% of your purchase amount up to a set limit.

Shops that require a purchase of services or other intangibles, such as salons, movie theaters, dry cleaners, auto repair shops, etc. will reimburse for a specified purchase. For example, when shopping a salon you might be reimbursed for a shampoo, cut and style or blow dry, but not for getting your hair colored or permed. An oil change would be paid for when shopping an auto repair center, but not a tune-up or new brakes.

Never assume that a purchase you make will be reimbursed. Always look at the shop instructions. If it is not clear to you what will be paid for, ask.

When you receive a fee in addition to your purchase reimbursement it may range from $5 or $10 to $20, $50 or more. The amount of the fee will depend on factors such as how much time is required to do the shop and complete the report and if any special expertise or training is required. You may receive a bonus for doing a rush job when someone else canceled, or for doing a shop which is hard to assign.

Fees for fee-only shops start at about $10 for a very simple shop and may go up to $20, $50, $100 or more. The fee is usually based on how much time you must spend doing the shop, how simple or complex the report is, if any special expertise or experience is required, and the difficulty of finding shoppers to do the assignment. For example, the fee for a bank shop might be anywhere in the above range, depending on what is required of the shopper.

Fees for narrative reports or reports requiring extensive comments are usually higher than for reports which require you to complete a check-off form with just a few comments. Video shoppers often receive higher fees than shoppers doing standard written reports. Even though a video shopper doesn't have to write a report, the special expertise and training required to complete a quality video shop commands a higher fee.

The Bottom Line

Because assignments can be infrequent, you will not get rich as a mystery shopper. However, if you want to get an occasional free meal or free merchandise and make some extra cash while doing something enjoyable, mystery shopping is for you. Many shoppers have reported that with a little effort, and by being flexible about the types of assignments they accept, they often make hundreds of dollars a month in cash and free meals and merchandise as part time mystery shoppers.

In addition, mystery shoppers are sometimes offered other types of jobs. Many of the companies that will hire you to mystery shop also do market research, merchandising and other work for their clients. You may be asked if you would like these assignments, too. These might involve things such as stocking displays, counting merchandise in stock, and conducting customer surveys and exit interviews. Many of these assignments pay by the hour, not by the job. While you are never under any obligation to accept an assignment, these jobs can provide you with additional work and increase your income.

Can You Make a Living as a Mystery Shopper?

Most shoppers do this part time or spare time as a way of making extra money. There are a few mystery shopping companies that hire full time shoppers to handle all the jobs in an area. Other companies don't offer full time work, but may have a lot of work for dependable shoppers in certain areas.

Most of the time, you won't be able to get enough work from one, two or even ten companies to keep you busy and make a full time income. There are shoppers who make a full time income by working with 50, 80, or more companies. They may not have assignments from each of those companies every month, but they are juggling assignments from many companies at the same time.

Making a full time income as a mystery shopper isn't easy. It takes tremendous organizational skills, and you have to be very motivated. You will have to be flexible about the types of shops you are willing to do. It helps to be open to accepting jobs other than mystery shops, such as audits and surveys or merchandising.

It helps to be flexible about how far you are willing to travel. One full time shopper said that she will accept assignments that may be 100 miles or more from her home. She lines up many shops to be done along the way, then spends the day driving along her route, doing all the scheduled shops. This shopper knows how much she needs to earn in a day to reach the income goal she has set for herself. She books shops that will pay her at least that much, plus cover her expenses (e.g., gas and other automobile costs, meals, etc.).

Full time mystery shopping is not realistic for the vast majority of mystery shoppers, but if you think you would like to shop full time, here are a few tips:

If you haven't mystery shopped before, apply to several companies and do some shops to be sure you enjoy the work and want to do it full time.

Contact the companies that say they hire full time shoppers and ask if they have openings.

Apply to every mystery shopping company you can find. Let them know you are interested in a heavy volume of shops and you are willing to be flexible about your availability, types of shops, areas shopped, etc.

Stay in touch with the companies and schedulers you have worked for, and let them know you are interested in a heavier work load. If you have done a good job for them, and they have more work available, they will probably try to steer assignments your way.

As your work load increases, set up a good organization system to keep track of your assignments. Make sure you confirm offered assignments promptly, allow yourself plenty of time to do the shops you've accepted, and submit your reports promptly.

Although full time mystery shopping is not possible (or even desirable) for most shoppers, it can be done. Be prepared to work very hard, and you may be able to make it work for you.

Mystery Shoppers and Taxes

This section addresses taxation information under the United States' tax code. If you are not subject to U.S. tax laws, consult your taxing authority to determine how your mystery shopping income will be handled.

When mystery shopping, you will most often work as an independent contractor. That means that the companies paying you don't withhold income taxes, Social Security taxes or Medicare taxes. *You* are responsible for making sure your taxes are paid. In general, the fees you receive for mystery shopping are taxable as ordinary income, and are subject to federal income taxes, state and local income taxes, Social Security taxes, and Medicare taxes.

The good news is that when you are a contractor you are treated as a small business and you can deduct certain expenses. These may include postage, mileage and car expenses, travel, office equipment, computer and Internet fees, and perhaps even some purchases made while you are mystery shopping. You might qualify to deduct some of your housing expenses if you have a home office.

If any of the companies you work for pay you at least $600 during a year, they are required to provide you with a 1099 form. This is similar to the W2 form you would receive from an employer, and you will receive it about the same time (i.e., about January of the following year). The information on the 1099 is also reported to the Internal Revenue Service, so if you don't account for the income you will be hearing from the IRS.

Companies which did not pay you at least $600 are not required to send a 1099 form, and they may not report to the IRS how much they paid you. Many mystery shoppers mistakenly believe this means they don't have to pay taxes on that income, so they don't report it.

To report your independent contractor income, you will file a Schedule C with your regular tax return. For instructions on record keeping, what expenses you may deduct, and how to complete Schedule C, contact the IRS and ask for their publications on small business taxes. You can also find these publications at your local library.

You may be required to file quarterly estimated taxes if you make a significant income as a shopper or from other independent contractor activities, and you don't have other income which is subject to withholding. If you or your spouse are employed full time and have taxes withheld from your income, and mystery shopping represents a small part of your income, this probably won't be an issue for you. For more information, call your local IRS office and ask for information about quarterly estimated taxes.

Tax regulations are always changing, so be sure to refer to IRS publications and other guides for current tax information. Consult your tax preparer for additional information about how your mystery shopping income and expenses should be reported.

TIP:

When applying online, print copies of the completed application, independent contractor agreement, and company information from each web site where you apply.

This is an easy way to keep a record of the companies to which you've applied and the terms of your agreements with the companies.

How to Get Started

Most of the time, mystery shoppers are hired by companies that specialize in performing mystery shops, not directly by the businesses that are mystery shopped. Because you will work for mystery shopping companies that serve many different clients, you may have the opportunity to evaluate businesses of all kinds.

You will find an extensive list of companies that hire mystery shoppers in Appendix A of this book. Most of the companies listed have an online application and prefer or require that you apply online. Assume that if a company has an online application, that is the way they want you to apply. It works better for everyone, as you don't have to print and mail anything and they don't have to re-enter all of your information into their computers.

Some companies (especially local or regional companies) may not be set up to take your application online and would prefer to receive a resume and letter of interest. In other cases, you may call and request an application packet which you complete and return to the company.

In general, most mystery shopping companies don't want you to call them. They are managing hundreds or thousands of shops and shoppers during a single month, and they don't have a lot of time to spend on the phone. Of course, most encourage you to call or email if you have questions about an assignment, but don't call to ask if they got your application, or when they will have an assignment for you. If they need you, they will be in touch.

Keep track of the companies you've applied to. You may think you will remember all of the applications you've submitted, but you won't. Don't waste your time by submitting multiple applications to the same companies. Each of the company listings in Appendix A has a space for you to write the date you applied to that company, so you can easily keep track that way. You may also want to jot notes about the companies next to their listings.

Applying Online

Let's start with completing online applications. In every area of mystery shopping, including the application, each company has its own policies and procedures. What is true one place is not necessarily true at another. That means that it is always important to read any instructions you are given, starting with how to complete the application.

The primary reason mystery shopping companies reject applicants is that they did not fully complete the application. Answer every question. If you are asked for a writing sample, provide it. Companies told me that as many as 20% to 25% of applicants don't make it through the first screening because they did not provide all of the information required.

When you apply for a typical job, there are legal restrictions regarding the types of questions employers can ask prior to hiring you. Because we are all used to those limitations, some of the questions asked on a mystery shopping application may seem odd or inappropriate. You may be asked your age, race, marital status, number of children and their ages, if you own a car, if you have pets, whether you wear glasses, etc. Some companies may make these questions optional, while others will require that you answer to be considered for shops.

The good news is that questions such as these are not asked in order to *exclude* you, they are asked in order to *include* you. Some assignments require shoppers to be over or under a certain age to match the demographics of the client's customers. They may need three couples each of a different race or ethnicity to test compliance with non-discrimination laws. Shoppers may have to be accompanied by children. If someone is going to mystery shop a pet grooming service, they need a pet.

You might be concerned about providing personal information, including a Social Security Number, over the Internet. It is unlikely that someone is going to intercept your data transmission, and many companies use a secure server, which encrypts the data, for greater security. The company may need your Social Security Number for tax reasons. If you refuse to provide it, some companies will automatically reject your application.

How do you know you can trust the company asking for the information? One big clue is whether the company is a member of the Mystery Shopping Providers Association (MSPA). Members are required to operate according to the Association's professional standards and ethics. You can verify whether a company belongs at the MSPA's web site: http://www.mysteryshop.org/. Members also may display the MSPA logo on their web sites.

Belonging to the MSPA is a strong sign that a company is honest, ethical and professional. However, many good, honest companies are not members. If you run across a company that is not a member of the MSPA, spend a little time looking around their web site. Does the site appear professional? Is there information about the company and its owners? What does the web site say about how the company operates? If you don't have a good feeling about the company, don't apply. Just go on to the next one.

Remember that a big part of your job as a mystery shopper is filling out report forms and writing comments and narratives. If you don't bother to do a good job on the application, why should they believe that you will be thorough and accurate in completing your reports?

Spelling, grammar and punctuation matter. When providing a writing sample, create it in your word processor and make sure you spell check it. Then cut and paste the sample into the application. Of course, you should carefully proofread all of your application to catch any mistakes before you submit the application. Some companies are more forgiving than others on these matters, but why handicap yourself by doing a less-than-excellent job?

Don't fill out the application in ALL CAPS or all lower case. Your keyboard has a shift key, so use it to properly capitalize the first word in each sentence, proper nouns, etc. Many people get sloppy when writing on the computer and drop letters, ignore punctuation, use abbreviations such as "u" for "you," and otherwise make mistakes which are not acceptable in a mystery shopping report. Don't do these things on your application, either.

Some companies with online applications will ask you to print and mail a copy of their Independent Contractor agreement, or they will ask for a handwriting sample or other documentation. If they request it, do it. And do it promptly. If you take weeks to do something simple like print, sign and mail a contract, how long will it take you to complete an assignment?

Applying by Phone or Mail

A few companies will ask only for basic information online, then mail an application packet for you to complete. Companies without an online application may want you to call or write for an application packet. If a company doesn't have a web site, a good way to apply to them is to send a one-page resume and one-page letter of interest (see examples starting on page 51) through the mail. Always include a self-addressed, stamped envelope when you send a resume to a mystery shopping company. It makes it easier for them to respond with a letter or application.

When they send an application packet, it may include an application, a demographic information form (where you give information about your age, marital status, etc.), an Independent Contractor agreement, and a sample shop form. The company may also include information about the types of shops they do, their standards, when and how you can expect to be paid, etc.

When you receive an application packet be sure to complete all forms and return them quickly, along with anything else they request, such as a photo or a handwriting sample. They keep track of when they sent it and when it was returned. If you take weeks or months to complete the application, it doesn't bode well for how you'll do on a shop.

Resume and Letter of Interest

If the entire application process is online, you won't need to send a resume. However, some of the companies you apply to online will send an application form to be completed. Others may ask that you send a resume and letter of interest. Sending a resume and letter of interest is a good way to approach companies that don't have an online application.

Even if you make all of your applications online and never need to send a paper resume, writing one is a useful exercise. The process gets you to focus on what your qualifications are, and when you are done you have the information you need to fill out your applications on one handy page.

When a company asks me to complete a paper application, I send a resume and letter of interest, too, with the idea that the more information I provide to "sell" myself to them, the more likely I am to get assignments. After all, once you've written the resume and letter of interest for the companies that want it, it's easy to run a couple of extra copies and send them out to others.

Send a self-addressed, stamped envelope when contacting a company by postal mail to request an application. Most mystery shopping companies receive a lot of requests and applications, so make it easy for them to respond to you and easy for them to work with you.

Show that you are a professional. Type (or computer generate) your resume and cover letter (unless they specify handwritten). Don't use hot pink paper. Your resume should be on white, beige or light gray paper.

One mystery shopping company told me they received a letter written on notebook paper *in crayon!* Maybe the writer thought it was a good way to make his letter stand out and get attention. Well, his letter did stand out, and he did get attention. What he didn't get was a job. Be a pro.

On the following pages you'll find samples of a resume and letter of interest. Yours shouldn't look exactly like these, of course, but they are provided as examples of the kind of information which should be included. Make your resume and cover letter reflect your experience and qualifications.

Remember that mystery shopping companies need to know where you can shop, when you can shop, a little about your background, and enough personal demographic information that the company can match you to shops (e.g., tell them if you are married, have kids, wear glasses, own a car, own pets, have hobbies, etc.). Many companies use zip codes to assign shops, so let them know what zip codes you are willing to shop in. You might list anywhere from three to ten zip codes on your resume or in your letter of interest. (Many of the online applications you complete will ask for zip codes, too.)

Keep your resume and cover letter to one page each. You don't need to list every job you ever had, but tell where you are currently working and describe your background.

Mystery shoppers can be male or female, young moms or "seasoned citizens", employed, self-employed, homemakers or retirees. You don't need a college degree or special training and experience. So whoever you are, put your resume together to put your best foot forward and get started now!

SAMPLE RESUME

**Merry Shopper
123 Main Street
Anytown, USA 23456
(123) 456-7890/(123) 456-7891 Fax
merry@shop.com**

- Experienced mystery shopper
- Extensive background in customer service
- [X] years' experience in [retail/hospitality/etc.]
- Excellent written and verbal communication skills
- Proficient in use of the personal computer, including Microsoft Word, Excel, Access and other programs.
- Reliable transportation
- Flexible availability - days, evenings and weekends
- Accessible by phone/voice mail, pager/cell phone
- Own a computer with email and Internet access
- Fax capabilities (send and receive) at home

Work History

[Provide your current employer's name and a brief description of your duties. You may list previous employers or provide a few sentences about your background. If you haven't worked outside the home for several years, your experience as a homemaker may be relevant.]

Educational Achievements

[Do you have a degree? Mention it. Have you taken courses or seminars in customer service, marketing, or writing? Mention them here, especially if they are recent.]

Personal Information

[Normally, it is not a good idea to list personal information on a resume. However, it could work *for* you as a mystery shopper. Mention if you are married, have children or pets, wear glasses, own a car, etc. This could qualify you for assignments with special requirements.]

SAMPLE LETTER OF INTEREST

Merry Shopper
123 Main Street
Anytown, USA 23456
(123) 456-7890 / (123) 456-7891 Fax
merry@shop.com

Dear Sir or Madam:

I am an experienced mystery shopper and I wish to apply to be a contract mystery shopper with your company. My resume is enclosed.

I have a flexible schedule which allows me to complete assignments days or evenings, weekdays or weekends. I have reliable transportation, and own a fax machine and a personal computer with full Internet access. My husband is sometimes available for assignments requiring a couple, and I am a pet owner.

Anytown is in the Houston metropolitan area. I am available for assignments in zip codes 23456, 23460, 23277, 23480 and 23478.

My work experience includes many years in technical and management positions requiring excellent communication skills. I also have several years' experience in retail and food service, including a position as Assistant Manager of a fast food outlet.

Thank you for considering my application. I can be contacted at the above number during day or evening hours. There is an answering machine to take messages if I am unavailable. My mobile phone number is 123-456-7897.

I look forward to hearing from you!

Sincerely yours,

Merry Shopper

Scams to Avoid

There is a lot of interest in mystery shopping these days, and it has brought the scam artists out of the woodwork. Legitimate mystery shopping companies are doing their best to drive the scammers out of business, so these are not as common as they were a few years ago.

Of course, there will always be new ways for scammers to try to separate you from your money. Whether you are online or offline, if your intuition makes you feel uneasy about a company, STOP! Especially watch out for the following:

Phone scams

At least one company has placed ads in the newspaper claiming you can make hundreds of dollars weekly as a mystery shopper. They have you call a number (local or long distance) which gives some information about mystery shopping, and then they tell you to call another number for more information. The first number gives a telephone access code, and tells you to call a number in the 809 area code. This is a number in the Caribbean, and you will be charged anywhere from $30 to $100 or even more. **Do not call any number in the 809 area code unless you know exactly who you are calling.** Many of these numbers are scams, not just the one(s) related to mystery shopping information.

Directory scams

A company offers to list you in a directory of mystery shoppers to be distributed to companies hiring

53

mystery shoppers. The only problem is that there is no directory, or the directory is not distributed to companies that hire shoppers. They just take the money and run.

There are legitimate directories and data bases that charge a fee to list shoppers. Although the shopper information is distributed to lots of mystery shopping companies, it doesn't mean that you will necessarily get work as a result of being listed. Of course, you could earn back the fee you paid if you got just one or two shopping assignments as a result of being in the directory. And the directory company may offer other benefits as well. Before paying to be included in a data base or directory, make sure you understand what you are paying for.

Company list scams

There are several companies offering lists of supposed mystery shopping companies, but in fact they are simply lists of market research companies, many of which have never done mystery shopping. Before buying any company list, ask how the list was obtained and how often it is updated.

The list of companies in this book was updated in March, 2002, just before we went to press. Each of the companies listed promotes themselves as a mystery shopping company hiring contract shoppers. The information given for each company came from information published by the companies on the Internet, from personal interviews with the companies, and from other reliable sources.

Being an Independent Contractor

Most mystery shoppers are independent contractors, not employees. What's the difference? As an independent contractor, you are treated as a small business. This has both advantages and disadvantages to you.

When you are an employee, the employer is responsible for withholding income taxes from your pay, and matching your Social Security (FICA) and Medicare taxes. As an independent contractor, you receive the full amount of your pay and you are responsible for paying any taxes due. You may be required to file quarterly estimated income tax returns. Independent contractors are usually not covered by unemployment and workers compensation laws, so are not eligible for benefits.

The good news is that you get many of the tax breaks available to businesses, because you are now a small business person. For example, you can deduct expenses you incur in earning your income, such as equipment purchased, postage, phone calls, etc. (Although you can't take the deduction if you were reimbursed by the mystery shopping company.) You can take a tax deduction for a mileage allowance or a portion of your total car expenses. You may be able to deduct a portion of your housing costs as a home office.

Independent Contractor Agreements

Who decides whether you are an employee or an independent contractor? The Internal Revenue Service has a set of guidelines that can be used to make that determination. The guidelines are subject to change, but indications that a worker is a contractor rather than an employee include when the worker:

> is paid by the job, not by the hour;
> set his or her own work hours;
> performs similar services for other persons or companies;
> furnishes his or her own materials, supplies and equipment;
> can realize a profit or loss; and
> can choose to accept or reject a job assignment.

As an independent contractor you will be asked to sign a contractor agreement. The agreement will include specific mention of many of these conditions. Don't panic if, for example, the agreement says that you understand you may make a profit or suffer a loss. It is highly unlikely that you will lose money working as a contract mystery shopper. The language is in the agreement so that the IRS will conclude you are a contractor and not an employee.

Standard provisions in an independent contractor agreement include that no employment relationship is established; that the company does not guarantee any minimum amount of work and you are not required to accept any assignment; and that the agreement may be terminated by either party at any time.

Many of the agreements you are asked to sign will contain similar provisions and language, but read each one carefully and keep a copy for yourself. It is a legal agreement and you can and will be held to its terms.

If you see a provision in a contractor agreement that makes you uncomfortable, don't agree to it. You may want to ask for clarification from the mystery shopping company or an attorney before signing. Of course, you can always refuse to sign an agreement. If you do so you won't be eligible for assignments from that company, but there are lots of other companies you can work with.

Instead of signing a physical piece of paper, you may become contracted by reading the agreement online, then clicking a button that says "I agree." Treat this as if you were actually signing the agreement. Read it carefully, print a copy, then click on "I agree."

Confidentiality and Non-Compete Clauses

The agreement will often address confidentiality. As a mystery shopper, you have access to confidential and proprietary information about the mystery shopping company and its clients. The company could suffer financial loss or damage to its client relationships if you were to divulge this information, so you are required to agree to keep all dealings with the company and its clients confidential.

This means that at a minimum, you shouldn't talk to others about specific mystery shopping jobs you've done, you should never share report forms, completed reports, training manuals or other materials with others, and you shouldn't talk about clients or compensation schedules of the mystery shopping company.

Some companies will include a non-compete clause in the agreement. This clause says that while you work for them, and for a specified period thereafter (usually one year), you agree not to enter into a mystery shopping or evaluation business.

The clause will probably be written to allow you to work for other mystery shopping companies. It is designed to prohibit you from starting your own business and going into competition against the mystery shopping company. Don't agree to this if you plan to start your own mystery shopping company. You may not take it seriously, but they do.

Working with More than One Company

Even if you are an excellent worker and make yourself available 24 hours a day, you won't necessarily get as many assignments as you would like from one company. A lot depends on how many clients the shopping company has in your area, how often they are shopped, and how many other shoppers are competing for these jobs.

To get more work, you should apply to more companies. Most companies will ask if you have ever worked as a shopper, but they won't care if you are currently working for someone else. These companies understand that the work they have to offer is sporadic, and they won't fault you for trying to get more jobs than they can offer.

If they ask, be honest. Tell them you are working for other companies because one company can not provide as much work as you would like.

Ethics

That brings us to the ethics of working for more than one company. While there is nothing wrong with accepting assignments from several companies, you must respect the confidentiality of the information you receive from each company.

Pay attention to the terms of the confidentiality agreements, or confidentiality clauses of independent contractor agreements, you signed when you applied. At a minimum, follow these guidelines:

Don't share information with anyone about a mystery shopping company's clients, or shops you have done for any mystery shopping company.

Don't send copies of blank report forms, sample reports, or completed reports from one company to another.

Don't share information about compensation with other mystery shopping companies, clients or other shoppers.

Don't give training materials or other documents you received from one company to another.

Don't gossip about the people or clients of any of the companies you work with.

Don't discuss the results of mystery shops directly with the client, unless you have been asked to do so by the mystery shopping company.

Don't post proprietary information about a mystery shopping company or client to an Internet message board, chat or forum.

If you are not sure whether it is ethical to divulge something you know, **DON'T DO IT!** It is always better to be safe than sorry.

Remember that this is a business and you are a professional. Take your responsibilities seriously.

Getting Assignments

Once your application has been accepted and your information has been entered into a company's data base, you are eligible to start receiving mystery shopping assignments. You may receive an assignment very soon after applying, or it may take three to six weeks before you get your first mystery shopping opportunity. Many companies schedule the bulk of their shops once a month, but shops are scheduled all through the month due to cancellations and new projects.

Don't expect to receive a lot of assignments right away. Some companies will never contact you because they don't have assignments available in your area. Others may be happy to send you all the work they can once they know that you can be depended on to do a good job, but they will probably only offer one or two assignments to begin. Companies will not start you out with a lot of assignments because they want to make sure that you will do your assignments and that you will do a good job with them before increasing your work load.

In a perfect world, you would know exactly which companies need shoppers in your area and you could focus your efforts on those companies. You will find that some companies list at their web sites the places they are actively seeking shoppers. However, that is always subject to change. A company may get a new client with locations in your town, or lose a client with a presence in your town. That will affect their need for shoppers.

What if you applied several weeks or months ago, and have never gotten an assignment? It probably means that they don't have a need for shoppers in your area right now. Should you contact them? Probably not. However, if you haven't heard from them in several months it is acceptable to send a brief email letting them know that you are still interested in shopping for them. Be sure to include your identifying information: name, address, phone number, where you are willing to shop, etc.

Notify the companies you applied to if your information changes. For example, if your name changes due to marriage or divorce, you move, you get a new phone number or area code, your email address changes, or your employment status or availability changes. Most companies don't want you to fill out a completely new application when this happens. You may be able to notify them by email or fill out an update form on the web. Check the company web sites to see how they prefer to receive updates.

How Shops Are Scheduled

Companies schedule assignments many different ways, including via the web, message boards, email, postal mail and telephone. A single company may use more than one method of scheduling shops.

Scheduling via Web Sites

Some companies want you to check their web site regularly and claim any shops you want to do. They may tell you what dates the site will list new shops, or they may send email to let you know that new shops have been added. It is your responsibility to check the web site and notify the company that you would like to do a shop.

The web site will have the specifics of the shop, such as the deadline, the client or type of shop, the fee and any reimbursement to be paid. These assignments are usually first come, first served, so you need to check the site early and often to claim shops.

Scheduling via Message Boards

There are several message boards on the Internet where mystery shopping companies and schedulers post available shops. Interested shoppers are asked to register at a web site or send email.

See the Internet Resources in Appendix C for information on accessing message boards. You can also find job postings at the MSPA web site at http://www.mysteryshop.org/.

Scheduling via Email

Mystery shopping companies and schedulers often send email to let shoppers know they have assignments available. For example, an email might be sent to all of the shoppers in Louisiana to let them know about available shops in the state.

The email will give the details of the shop, such as location, type of shop, due date, fees and reimbursements, etc. Email is often used to reschedule shops that were canceled by another shopper, so they may be rush jobs. In that case, a bonus or incentive may be offered to get the job done quickly.

These assignments are also filled on a first come, first served basis, so to have the best chance at these assignments, check your email often.

Scheduling via Postal Mail

Some companies will send assignments through the mail, usually to shoppers who have worked for them before. The shopper is required to confirm that they received the shop and accept or decline it.

Postal mail is used less than it used to be, as more companies use email and the web to schedule; however, you may still receive assignments this way.

Scheduling via Telephone

Telephone scheduling may be used when a company needs to find a replacement shopper quickly for someone who has canceled. Or, you may receive your first assignment from a company by phone, so that they can talk with you before assigning the shop. Telephone scheduling isn't done often, but some shops are still scheduled over the phone.

What to Do When You Are Contacted

Whenever you are contacted by a mystery shopping company, follow their instructions. You generally aren't expected to respond to an email that is sent to all of the shoppers in an area announcing a shop, unless you want to be considered for the shop.

However, if an email is sent specifically to you offering a shop, respond as soon as possible.

The same thing goes for any other contact. If you are called about a shop, or receive an assignment in the mail, you are expected to respond as soon as you can. Never let it go more than 24 hours, and respond sooner if you can.

Once You're Confirmed

When you have accepted a shop and been confirmed, the mystery shopping company will send you detailed instructions for completing the shop. They may fax, email or mail forms, instructions and sample reports to you. If the report is to be completed online, you'll be told where to log in to get your instructions and submit your report.

Working with Schedulers

In addition to working with schedulers who are on staff at a mystery shopping company, you may receive assignments from independent schedulers. These are people who are typically contractors who are hired to assign the shops and make sure they are completed.

From a mystery shopper's perspective, working with independent schedulers is about the same as working directly with the mystery shopping company's schedulers. The advantage of working with these independent schedulers is that they may work with several mystery shopping companies. They use the data base of shoppers who have applied to the mystery shopping company, as well as their own data bases of shoppers.

By working with schedulers, you may get shops from companies you have never worked with or applied to before. And, just like the staff schedulers at mystery shopping companies, if an independent scheduler knows that she can count on you to do a good job, she will send jobs your way when she can.

You will find schedulers listed in the Mystery Shopping Directory in Appendix A.

Organization and Record Keeping

As a mystery shopper, you may be responsible for completing many assignments during the course of a month. You may work for multiple mystery shopping companies and shop several clients for each.

Each evaluation may have a different time period in which it is to be done. Each client will have a different report format, and there may be unique requirements for each shop you do.

When you are a professional mystery shopper you have to juggle a variety of assignments and keep track of income and expenses for tax purposes. If you are not organized, it is easy to miss deadlines or forget to do things you are supposed to do. If you haven't kept track of your finances during the year, preparing your taxes can take longer than it should, and you may miss out on deductions you didn't record.

Fortunately, organizing your mystery shopping assignments doesn't have to be complicated. When you first start, and you're doing just a few assignments, mark them on the calendar and put the paperwork with other important papers (such as bills to be paid).

As the number of assignments available to you increases, you can set up a system that works for you. One easy was to do this is to get a file box and some file folders. Set up a folder for each assignment, and put all the paperwork for that assignment in the folder. The paperwork might include the assignment confirmation, instructions, report forms, etc. Folders may be sorted by mystery shopping company, due date, or whatever works for you.

Keep track of due dates on a calendar reserved for that purpose. A large desktop calendar, with lots of room to write on it, works well.

Enter each shop in your computer as it is assigned to you. A data base program or spreadsheet, such as Microsoft Excel, works well. Include the name of the mystery shopping company and client, location, due date, fee, reimbursement, etc. You can use this file to monitor which shops you haven't completed, which you have, and track payments as they are received.

Keep copies of completed reports and receipts at least until you have been paid for them. That way, if there are any questions about the report or a receipt is lost in the mail, you can easily locate the information and resolve the problem.

Make a log of your auto mileage so you can claim any allowable mileage deductions on your tax return. A small notebook you keep in your car works well. Note the date, the purpose of your trip and the miles for each trip.

Other expenses can be recorded in a notebook or on your computer. Use envelopes or file folders to hold receipts for any business purchases.

Your record keeping system doesn't have to be complicated. It just has to work for you. You may want to experiment with different methods until you hit on the one you like best.

Preparing for the Shop

Review your shop instructions as soon as you receive them. If you are asked to confirm the shop, do it immediately. You can also take that opportunity to ask any questions you have about the instructions.

If this is the first time you've shopped for this company, or the first time you've shopped this client, the mystery shopping company may want you to call for training over the phone. It gives them a chance to remind you of the most important aspects of the shop and make sure you understand what is required.

There may be things you have to do before going to the location, such as making a reservation or an appointment, or completing a telephone shop. Allow time to do these tasks before making the visit.

Read the instructions and report form very carefully before going to the location. Make sure you understand them completely and know what you are to do. This is the time to ask questions. Use a highlighter to identify key issues of the shop.

Don't take the form with you to do the mystery shop. Instead, make a "cheat sheet" by making a reduced copy you can tuck in a pocket or purse, or make a few notes you can discreetly refer to during the shop.

If you are allowed or required to take someone with you on the shop, make sure they know what they are expected to do. Is there something they should or shouldn't ask? Will they help you with the shop by reading name tags or timing something? Or is their job to not get in the way while you do the shop? Go over their responsibilities carefully so that there are no mistakes and you get a valid shop.

Training

The training you receive will vary from one company (and one client) to the next. You will always receive written instructions on doing the shop. Some companies provide detailed manuals with all of their policies and procedures and everything you need to know about shopping for them.

Companies may want to conduct a telephone training session with you, especially the first time you do a shop for them. It gives you the chance to ask any questions, and they can feel confident that you understand what is required of you.

In some circumstances you will receive face-to-face training. This might involve meeting with someone at an office, classroom training where you are trained along with other shoppers, or field training where you go into a business and conduct an actual shop or a test shop with your trainer.

Whatever form your training takes, make sure you understand what you are supposed to do. If you have questions at any point in the process, ask for clarification. They want you to ask questions about anything you are not sure of.

Sample
Report Questions

Each mystery shopping report will address the issues important to that client. Shops done for one client will be different than shops done for another, even if you are working for the same mystery shopping company each time.

Some of the questions may seem unimportant to you, but they are all important to the client. Each one is there for a reason, so before you do the shop spend some time getting familiar with the evaluation form and what the client wants you to look for.

It may seem like a lot to remember (and it is), but after you've done a few mystery shops you will find that it gets easier. For example, almost every report form will ask questions about cleanliness. Get used to noticing if doors and windows are free of dirt and fingerprints, floors are clean and dry, counters and tables are wiped clean, displays are neat and orderly, etc. Expect that you will check the rest room to see if it is clean and fully stocked.

Once you are accustomed to checking these basics every time you do an evaluation, your preparation can focus on any questions which are specific to the client you are preparing to shop. For example, in addition to verifying that the rest room is clean and stocked, the client for today's shop might want to know if there is a maintenance schedule posted on the rest room door, and if it is indicates that the rest room has been inspected and cleaned hourly.

The following pages list typical questions you can expect to see on mystery shopping report forms. These questions are not taken from any particular company's forms, but represent common issues addressed by mystery shopping.

Generic Questions

These questions might be found on the report forms when mystery shopping almost any type of business.

Day of the week shop completed.

Date and time of day.

Weather conditions (hot or cold, sunny or rainy, etc.).

Could you easily find a parking space?

Was the parking lot clear of loose carts and litter-free?

Were sidewalks clean and litter-free?

Was landscaping attractive and well-maintained?

Was the entrance clean?

Were the windows clean and free of fingerprints?

Were you greeted within 30 seconds of entering?

Were aisles clear? Floors clean and free of debris?

Was background music at a comfortable level?

Which rest room did you visit—Men's or Women's?

Was the rest room clean?

Was the rest room properly stocked with tissue, soap and towels or hand dryer?

How many cashiers/check-out lines were available?

How many people were ahead of you at the cashier? Name of cashier.

Was your order rung up correctly by the cashier?

Did the cashier state the total of your purchase?

If paid by check or charge, did cashier address you by name at any time during the transaction?

If paid with cash, did cashier count your change back to you?

Were you offered a receipt?

Total time required to check out.

Based on your experience today, would you return to this place of business?

What you did you like best about your visit?

What suggestions for improvement would you make?

Fast Food Restaurants

How many counter persons were taking orders?

How many people were waiting in line?

Was counter person in uniform? Neat and well-groomed?
     Name of counter person:

Did counter person repeat your order to verify it?

Did counter person use suggestive selling (e.g., ask if you wanted dessert)?

Was the total correct?

Was correct change given?

Did counter person say thank you?

Were tables/counters/floors clean?

Was condiment station fully stocked and clean?

Was your food served as ordered?

Were food and beverages delicious?

Was a manager visible during your visit?

Were tables cleared and cleaned with 90 seconds of customer departure?

Sit-Down Restaurants

How long did you wait to be seated?

How long after you were seated did server greet you?
Name of server:

Did server tell you about the daily special?

Did s/he suggest a specific appetizer?

Were all glasses/silver/plates and bowls clean?

Was your food prepared as ordered?

Was your food attractively presented?

Were all food items delicious?

Was hot food hot and cold food cold?

Did the server check back with you within two minutes after your food was served?

Were used dishes removed during your meal?

Were you offered coffee and dessert?

Was a manager visible during your visit?

Were tables bussed within three minutes after customer departure?

Retail Stores

Were you greeted when you entered the store?

Were shopping carts readily available?

Were sale fliers available near the entrance?

Was the service desk neat and orderly (not piled with merchandise)?

Was a manager visible? What was s/he doing?
  Manager's Name:

Could you easily find the item(s) you were instructed to shop for?

Were advertised items in stock?

Were prices displayed?

Did displayed prices match prices charged?

Was merchandise displayed neatly?

Was signage neat (no handwritten signs)?

Were aisles clear?

How many associates came within 10 feet of you?
  How many greeted or acknowledged you?

Ask a sales associate for directions to an item. Did the associate:

Take you to the item?

Hand the item to you?

Ask if you needed additional assistance?

Associate's name:

Ask an associate a product-knowledge question. Did the associate:

Answer your question satisfactorily, or get an answer for you?

Ask if you need any other assistance?

Was the associate polite?

Was the associate neat and well-groomed?

Associate's name:

How many checkouts were open?

Were more than three customers in any line?

How long did you wait in line?

Did the cashier:

Greet you?

Make eye contact?

Smile?

Ring your order correctly?

Scan each individual item?

Count your change back?

Offer a receipt?

Say thank you?

Cashier's Name:

Doing a Mystery Shop

Make sure you are thoroughly prepared before going to the location. Be certain to do the shop during the time frame required. If the shop is to be done between the 1st and the 10th of the month, do it then. If it is supposed to be done during certain hours of the day (e.g., dinner, between 5:30 and 7:30 p.m.) be sure to go at that time. And make sure you go to the right location. Double check the business name and the address.

What to Look For

The report form and instructions tell you what to look for when doing the shop. You may be told to go to a certain department and ask questions about the merchandise, or check items to see if they are in stock.

You will usually go into the rest room to see if it is clean and well-stocked. In a restaurant, you may time how long before your order is taken, or until you got your food. You will check for safety hazards, such as puddles of water on the floor or merchandise stacked in the aisles.

How many cashiers were available? How many people were in line ahead of you? Is the facility clean?

Did the salesperson offer you the extended warranty? You will get the names or descriptions of the employees you dealt with.

Each of the questions on the report form is there because the client needs to know about that aspect of his business. Make sure you get the information to answer each question accurately and completely. But don't stop there. If you notice something that isn't asked about on the form, whether it's good or bad, make a note of it. Remember to keep all comments objective. This is not about your personal taste and opinions.

One of the myths about mystery shopping is that the shopper is looking for what is wrong. Some think that if they haven't found a lot of "bad stuff" they haven't done their jobs as mystery shoppers. In fact, your job is to give an objective picture of your experience at the business.

Unless instructed otherwise, you shouldn't try to trick the employees being evaluated, or make it hard for them to do what they are supposed to do. Nor should you make it too easy by leading them to do the right thing. Think of yourself as a camera, recording what is happening. Do your best not to influence the outcome of a shop, either positively or negatively, with your behavior.

If the experience was great, that's good news. Most of the questions you are asked in your report call for objective answers. You are not writing a review, you are describing what happened—so tell it like it is, with the good, the bad, and the ugly!

When You Arrive

The shop begins before you've gotten out of your car. The report may include questions about the condition of the parking lot and building exterior, for example. If you can't be observed by employees, you may note the answers on your form before you get out of the car.

It's also a good idea to make a quick review of the form just before you go in. Read the items you highlighted to remind yourself what information you need to get. Check to see that you have your cheat sheet tucked away in your pocket or purse. Make sure your watch is ready to time anything you need to time, and make a note of what time you are entering the business.

Getting Names

Most shops require that you get the names of the employees you observed. That can be easy if they are wearing name tags. Of course, you should be subtle about reading name tags. Don't stare or make a big deal about it. One shopper leaves her sunglasses on for the first few minutes, so employees can't tell where she is looking. Once she gets the names, she removes her sunglasses.

If an employee is not wearing a name tag, you may be able to get his or her name in another way. The receipt often gives the name of the cashier. You may hear the employee addressed by name by a customer or another employee. Be creative and you can often come up with a way to ask. For example, ask your server his name so you can ask for him next time you're in.

When you can't get a name, be sure to get a good description. Some reports will ask for description even if you have the name. Gender, race, height, weight, hair color and style, and distinguishing characteristics such as glasses or a beard can all be used to identify someone. Don't describe them using unflattering or insensitive descriptions, such as fat, foreign, etc.

Taking Notes or Using a Recorder

As you can tell, there is a lot to include in your reports. You probably won't be able to recall it all without making some notes as you do the shop (especially when you are new at this). Be discreet about making notes while you are doing the shop. Employees know that mystery shoppers are used, and if they know they are being shopped you won't get an accurate picture.

You will almost always have to check the rest room. That is a good place to make notes about what you have observed to that point, and review your cheat sheet to remind yourself what else you need to do.

When doing a retail shop, you may be able to carry a shopping list and make notes there.

Sometimes you will be asked to tape record the shop. This is especially true when you are having a long conversation with an employee (e.g., an apartment rental agent, banker, etc.). You may also choose to discreetly use a recorder during other shops.

During a shop, you might be able to use the pay phone or your mobile phone to call your home answering machine and leave a message with names or other observations you need to have for your report.

Of course, you should only do this if you are certain you won't be overheard by employees.

Several companies are now using hidden video cameras to record the entire shop. This is especially true when the client wants to see and hear what the employee did during a presentation, such as for home builders, apartment complexes, banks and car dealerships. However, video shopping is used for retail, restaurant and other shops as well. If you are asked to videotape the shop, the company will provide the equipment and train you on how to use it. The equipment is so small that a camera may be hidden in a button or a piece of jewelry. The best part about videotaping a shop is that you won't have to write a report!

Taking Someone with You

You may want to take your spouse, child or friend with you when you are mystery shopping. Make sure that it is allowed before taking anyone along on a shop.

When asked, "May mystery shoppers bring their children along on shops?" the answers given by mystery shopping companies ranged from, "Yes," to "Sometimes," to "Never!" You should never take *anyone* along with you if they will be a distraction or interfere with the shop in any way.

There may even be times when you are asked to take your children or someone else with you, because of a client requirement. However, if the shop instructions say you should go alone, or say not to bring children, follow those instructions. The instructions for restaurant shops often suggest or require that you have a companion. If you want to take your children, contact the mystery shopping company and make sure children are allowed before you do so.

In general, you may be able to take your children on a shop if it is a place you would normally take them (for example, to a fast food restaurant, but probably not fine dining). Never assume that your children are welcome to accompany you on a shop. Always ask the mystery shopping company.

Whenever someone accompanies you on a shop, it is your responsibility to see that they know what to do. Explain the important instructions to them before you go. For example, you might be asked not to order an appetizer until your server has had a chance to suggest one. If the first words out of your companion's mouth are, "Bring us an order of fried cheese," you haven't followed the shop instructions.

Your companion must also understand the need for secrecy. They must not do anything to give away the fact that you are mystery shopping.

Remember That You Are a "Mystery" Shopper

When you are doing a shop, you must not let anyone know that you are a mystery shopper. The whole idea is that you want to see how the typical customer is treated. If they know you are a mystery shopper, you will not have a typical experience.

Don't tell anyone who works for the store that you are mystery shopping, and don't talk about mystery shopping with any companions you have. If you have children with you, don't tell them you are doing a mystery shop if they are likely to share this information with anyone who happens to be around.

Don't carry your report form with you. Some companies will provide a cheat sheet which you can fold up and carry to remind you of what you need to do on the shop. Be discreet when you take any notes. Many times, you can carry a shopping list and make your notes there.

You may feel very conspicuous, especially the first few times you go mystery shopping. It may seem to you that you have a large neon sign on your forehead, flashing MYSTERY SHOPPER. In fact, no one will know that you are a mystery shopper.

I've had to ask questions or do things that I was sure would alert all the employees that I was checking up on them. In reality, no one noticed or thought anything about it. The employees know that their location is mystery shopped; however, they often don't know exactly what the mystery shopper will do or ask. And, frankly, real shoppers will do odder things than we are asked to do!

If you are really concerned about it, construct a couple of possible scenarios ahead of time, and plan how you would deal with them. For example, what would you say if an employee asked if you are a mystery shopper? It's not going to happen, but if you're worried about it, plan a response.

One answer would be, "No, I'm not." The best way to handle it is probably to act like you've never heard of mystery shopping. You will end the questioning quickly by asking, "Mystery shopper? What's that?"

I did a number of shops where I was required to return something I had purchased only minutes before. I was certain that at worst, they would immediately know I was a mystery shopper, and at best, they would think it was odd. Therefore, I concocted all sorts of stories as to why I was returning items I'd just bought: I thought this purse would match the shoes I bought at another store, I picked up the wrong size, etc. *They never asked any questions, they just processed my return.* So, while you should try not to draw attention to yourself, don't be overly concerned about being identified as a mystery shopper.

Telephone Mystery Shopping

You may be asked to do some shops by telephone. For example, a hotel chain or airline might want to evaluate its reservations agents, an insurance company its claims staff, or a mail order company its phone order takers. Telephone shops are often a part of restaurant, bank and retail shops, too.

Just as in the in-person shops, you will have a list of questions to answer. You may be able to complete the report while you are on the phone, from memory or your notes after you hang up, or you may tape the call.

Questions which may be included in a telephone shop include:

How many rings before you received an answer?

Did you have to make more than one attempt before getting a ring?

Was the phone answered by a person or a recorded message?

Did the person who answered give their name? Name:_____

How long were you on hold?

Ask (assigned question). Was the associate able to answer your question?

Was the associate courteous? Did s/he sound like s/he was smiling?

Did the associate encourage you to come in?

Did s/he thank you for calling?

Video Mystery Shopping

Have you ever imagined yourself going undercover, like one of those TV reporters with a hidden camera? That is very much what it is like when you do a video mystery shop.

During a video mystery shop you will do many of the same types of things you do in a regular mystery shop. You will ask questions of employees, engage them in conversations and record their responses. You may also be asked to record images of the sales floor and service areas.

An advantage of video over written reports is that the client can see exactly what happened, and not have to rely on the written impressions of the mystery shopper. The employee who was shopped can view the tape and see exactly how they come across to customers.

The video equipment is easily hidden. The camcorder and battery pack are usually worn on a belt or carried in a purse. The camera itself it so small that it can be hidden in a button or a piece of jewelry.

Shoppers hired to do video shopping often have experience in mystery shopping or using video equipment. If you are asked to do a video mystery shop, you will be trained on how to use the equipment and conduct the shop.

Training is usually conducted in person. You may be asked to do some sample or test shops to get used to using the equipment. According to the companies that do video shopping, the best way to learn is to do a shop then view the tape you made. You can immediately see your results that way. Test shops allow you to learn without the pressures of a real shop.

The mystery shopping company will provide the video equipment for you. You may pick it up from a local location or it will be shipped to you. One company said their goal is to have a network of shoppers who own their own equipment. They will receive higher fees (because the equipment won't have to be shipped to them) and they may even be able to rent the equipment for use by other shoppers.

Video mystery shoppers often receive higher fees than mystery shoppers doing a standard written report. Fees start at about $30 and can go up to $150 or more.

Dealing with Problems

You accepted the shop, but now you can't do it, or you can't do it on time. Perhaps you did the shop but you forgot to get a business card from the employee you spoke with. Or you lost the receipt. Or your computer crashed and you can't complete the report. What should you do?

First of all, contact the mystery shopping company or scheduler by email or phone to let them know about the problem. Tell them what you can and can't do, then let them decide how to handle the situation.

When you can't do a shop you've accepted because of an emergency, they will reschedule it with another shopper. By telling them as soon as possible, you give them time to get the job done.

Don't ask someone else to do the shop in your place. The mystery shopping company contracted with you, and your shop usually can not be assigned to someone else. However, if you know someone who could fill in for you, you may suggest them to the mystery shopping company.

If you can't make a deadline, the company may be able to extend it by a day or two. Don't rely on this month after month, but in a real emergency they can probably work with you. I once had to do this because of car trouble on the day the shop was scheduled. I immediately called the mystery shopping company, let them know about the problem and that I was getting the car fixed that day. I offered to do the shop first thing the following morning and get the report to them immediately afterward. They were understanding and allowed me to do the shop the next day. Had I not called, and waited for them to call me asking for the report, they would not have been as understanding.

You may be required to submit a receipt or business card from the shop along with your report. If something happened to it, or you forgot to get it, contact the company and ask how they want to handle it. Don't just submit the report without the receipt and hope they don't notice. They will. Be honest and up front with them and you may be able to salvage the situation.

Many reports are now done on the computer in Word or Excel, or via the Internet, so a computer crash can be a real problem. When reports are done on the web, you can access the Internet through another computer (such as a friend's or one at the library) and complete your report that way. If the report forms crashed with your computer, contact the company and ask what they want you to do.

Bottom line: Whenever there is a problem, contact the mystery shopping company or scheduler, let them know what happened and let them decide what should be done. If you can offer a solution, do so; but they will decide how it will be handled.

Avoiding Problems

Stuff happens, and anyone can make a mistake or have an emergency pop up. Although companies will be understanding in an emergency, if you seem to have a problem on every assignment the assignments will stop coming. A few simple steps can help you to avoid the situations described above.

Keep good records of your assignments, so you know what is due and when. "I forgot" is not considered a valid excuse for missing a deadline.

When scheduling shops, remember your other commitments. One shopper canceled an assignment at the last minute saying she "forgot Christmas was in December." Not good.

Do your shops early. When you have a window of time to complete the assignment, plan to do the shop as early as possible. That way, if something goes wrong you still have time to get it done by the deadline.

Review all instructions and requirements carefully before doing the shop to minimize the possibility of forgetting to do part of the evaluation, or not getting documentation you need, such as a receipt or business card.

Write the report as soon as you finish the shop, and send receipts immediately, before you have a chance to lose them.

Back up your computer files regularly so that if you have a crash you can get up and running quickly.

Have contingency plans in place. Think about the "what ifs" and come up with solutions you can implement if they become reality.

Writing the Report

Once you've done the shop, the next step is to complete your report. Don't be surprised if it takes longer than you expected to do your first reports. Like most things, it will get easier with experience.

The time required to complete your report may range from a few minutes for a simple check-off form with a few comments, to hours for an extensive narrative. Although your fee is not usually expressed as an hourly rate, companies consider the relative ease or difficulty of completing the report, and the time that may be required, when setting fees.

Before writing your report, gather anything you need: forms to complete, log-in information if the forms are online, notes or tapes you made during the shop, the instructions and/or sample reports, receipts or other documents, etc.

Do it Now!

The report should be written immediately after completing the shop, while your memories are strong. Some sections of the report may be completed while you are doing the shop, others will be constructed from memory or from the notes you took or by listening to a tape recording.

What to Include

Some companies will provide a sample report to illustrate how the report should be completed, the number of comments to include and the level of detail to include in the comments. If you receive a sample, follow the format as closely as possible but don't copy the words exactly. While some clients love having lots of comments, others want very few. The sample will give you an idea of what they expect.

All of the information you provide should be as objective as possible. You are reporting what happened, not writing a review. Don't say the food was bad, say why. Was it cooked improperly? Cold? Stale? Not what you ordered? Be specific. Don't say that the food was poorly prepared because you don't happen to like the flavor.

Don't say the wait was "too long", say you waited 10 minutes before you reached the cashier. Saying the manager was helpful isn't very clear. Saying that you saw him carry trays for a mother dining with three small children tells exactly what happened.

Use names or descriptions of employees. The client wants to know who is doing a great job, and who is doing a not-so-great job. Telling him is *your* job.

Answer each question on the form. Add comments to back up both positive and negative ratings. Make sure that your answers are consistent with your comments. If you answer a question that, yes, the salesperson served you promptly, but in your comments say that you had to wait five minutes while he finished a personal call, that doesn't add up!

Remember that you're giving an objective picture of what you saw, and you're not trying to find things wrong. Don't look for excuses to give a poor rating. Be honest and fair. One tissue on the rest room floor doesn't mean that the rest room wasn't clean. (C'mon, you know right away when a rest room isn't clean, don't you?) Of course, if the instructions for the shop say that any flaw is reason for a "no" answer, follow the instructions.

If you are not sure how to answer a question, email or call the mystery shopping company and ask. Let's say the evaluation form asks if the salesperson offered you the Premium Gold Maintenance Plan. Your salesperson told you a service contract is available, but didn't specifically mention the Premium Gold Maintenance Plan by name. Do they get a yes or a no? That depends on the company's service standard. When in doubt, contact the mystery shopping company and ask.

Keep your comments objective, and focused on what you observed. Don't tell them what they should do, tell them what you saw. For example, don't say that the floor "needed to be mopped." Say that the floor was dirty, especially the baseboards and in the corners, or that there was a puddle of standing water about 12" wide. Instead of "trash needed to be emptied" say that the trash can was overflowing onto the floor if that's what you saw.

If you are required to do a narrative report, you will be told what you must include, and how long the report should be at minimum or maximum. Follow the guidelines as closely as possible.

Some companies will appreciate it if you go beyond the questions you are required to answer in a form or narrative report, and mention anything notable. Did you see an employee go out of his way to help a customer? Was the sneeze guard missing from the salad bar? Was a loose tile causing a safety hazard? Provide any observations that you might want to know about if you owned that business.

Because most reports are now completed using a computer, it is unlikely that you will be asked to handwrite your report. However, if anything is handwritten, your writing must be neat and legible.

Your reports must be organized and easy to follow. Put comments in the correct locations. You may be asked to number your comments to correspond to the questions on the form. Whatever the instructions, make sure you follow them.

Don't assume that because you have been mystery shopping for a while, or because you have mystery shopped for the same company or client before, that you know what to do. Always read and follow the instructions. Requirements vary from one client to the next, and even from one shop to the next for the same client.

Before submitting your report, check it over to make sure it is complete and correct. Look for unanswered questions, data entry errors, misspelled words, missing or inconsistent comments, or anything else that will cause the mystery shopping company to call you. If your report is incomplete, your fee may be reduced or withheld. A pattern of poor reports means you won't receive future assignments.

Sample Narrative Report

The sample report on the next two pages is provided to give you an idea of what a narrative might look like and what kind of information may be included.

This report is only an example. If you are required to write a narrative report be sure to follow the guidelines you are given regarding length, level of detail, specific issues to address, etc.

Sample Narrative Report

Restaurant: Mama's Hacienda
Location: My Town, USA

Day: Thursday   Date: Sept. 27
Time of visit: 6:15 p.m. - 7:10 p.m.

My guest and I entered the restaurant and were immediately approached by a hostess (Monica). She greeted us, asked our seating preference, and seated us at a booth in the non-smoking section, as requested.

Jason greeted us 30 seconds after we were seated and brought water, chips and salsa to the table. He also offered green sauce.

Our waiter, Miguel, arrived within two minutes and asked for our drink order. We ordered margaritas, and he asked if we preferred our drinks frozen or on the rocks. Miguel suggested the Amazin' Onion appetizer, and we ordered one.

The drinks (frozen) were served in frosted mugs, with salt around the rims and a lime wedge garnish. They were thick enough that the straws stood up in the mugs, but we were able to drink them through the straws. The margaritas were properly tart, but we could not taste any tequila in them.

The Amazin' Onion was presented on a platter with a dipping sauce in the center. The batter on the onion was soggy, not crisp, but the flavor was good.

I ordered the Cheeseburger Platter. The burger was served open-faced, with lettuce, tomato and onion. A pickle and french fries filled the rest of the platter. The burger was prepared as ordered, and was cooked as specified. The burger and french fries were hot, and the garnish and pickle were cold and crisp. The bun was fresh, the beef of high quality, and the fries crisp and golden.

My companion ordered the Gringo Special, which included a taco, a burrito and an enchilada, with sides of rice and beans. The appearance of the plate was excellent, with the food presented in an appetizing and colorful way. All food was served hot, except the lettuce, onion and tomato garnishes which were cold and crisp. The food was all excellent, except the refried beans, which were watery.

Our used plates were cleared promptly by Miguel and Jason during the meal. Additional drinks were offered, and water glasses were refilled often. All food portions were generous. We asked for extra napkins and were given several.

Miguel returned to ask for our dessert order. He presented the dessert tray and knowledgeably answered our questions. We selected the chocolate cake and the raspberry cheesecake. Both were served in generous portions and had excellent flavor.

Miguel brought the check as we finished our dessert. I paid by credit card, and he returned promptly with my receipt. As we left, both Miguel and Monica thanked me by name.

My guest and I agreed that we had a pleasurable dining experience, and we would return to Mama's Hacienda.

Getting Paid

Payment procedures are explained when you are hired or in the instructions you receive for the shop. Some mystery shopping companies will pay you automatically based on your submission of a completed report and receipt or other documentation. Others want you to submit an invoice along with the report. The mystery shopping company can not invoice the client without complete information from you, so you won't be paid if you don't submit a complete report, receipt and any other documentation required for the shop.

If you do not complete the job as instructed, and within the time required you may not be paid (or your pay could be reduced), so be sure to follow all instructions carefully. Some companies will reduce your pay if they have to call you about an incomplete report or extensive editing is required. Others will pay a bonus when you do excellent work and submit reports promptly. All of this will be explained when you receive your assignment.

Once you have submitted your report, you will be paid during the company's usual payroll cycle. That could mean you get paid in a few days, a few weeks or the following month. The company will tell you their payroll cycle when you are hired or when you accept an assignment. Typically, you will be paid within three to five weeks of completing the shop, with some payments coming sooner, a few later.

It is a good idea to keep a record of the shops you do for each mystery shopping company, the fees and reimbursements due, and the dates services were rendered. Record the payment when it is received.

By recording your shops and payments in this way you will always know exactly how much you are owed, or if the account is paid in full. Once in a while something happens to a check (e.g., your paperwork is misplaced, the check goes astray in the mail, etc.) and you want to make sure you receive all of your pay.

You can use a spreadsheet, data base or accounting program on your computer to keep track of your fees. This will also simplify pulling together the information you need for your tax return.

Working with Mystery Shopping Companies

Once you start receiving assignments you will want to do the best job you can so that companies continue to send you mystery shopping opportunities, and perhaps increase the number of shops you are offered.

When you do a good job, companies will happily offer you more work if they can. The mystery shopping companies I surveyed all said that they have shoppers they employ as often as possible because they are dependable and do excellent work. There are also shoppers they would love to give more assignments to, but they simply don't have enough clients in the shopper's area to do so. And, of course, there are shoppers they won't work with again because they didn't do the job they were given.

Even though some companies may not be able to work with you as much as you and they would like, you will probably find that there are a least a couple of companies that have a large number of shops available in your area. Doing your best work will keep them sending you all the assignments they can.

Doing Your Best

The three most important things to remember about doing a mystery shop are:

Do it on time.
Do it completely.
Do it accurately.

On time means that the shop is completed and your report submitted by (or before) the deadline.

Completely means that you have provided all required information, filled in all of the spaces on the form, and made appropriate comments. Also remember to attach any required documentation, such as a receipt.

Accurately means that the shop was done on the correct day and at the proper time, the information you provided is correct, the ratings correlate with your comments, and the report is the best work you can possibly do.

The fourth and most important point: *do it.* If you accept, but do not complete an assignment, it is likely that you will not receive another assignment from that company. If an emergency comes up that keeps you from completing your assignment, or keeps you from getting your report in on time, call the company *immediately* to let them know.

Dos and Don'ts

Following these suggestions will keep you in good graces with mystery shopping companies and schedulers, and will help you go to the front of the line for more and better assignments.

Do communicate with the mystery shopping companies you work with and let them know about anything that will affect getting your reports done on time.

Don't call them just to chat. They don't have time.

Do drop them an email to let them know if there has been a change in your contact information or availability.

Don't badger them about when they will have a job for you, or why they don't give you more assignments. That's a sure way to get no assignments in the future!

Do complete your assignments as soon as possible during the shopping period.

Don't ask for extra time to complete your assignments, month after month.

Do respond promptly when a mystery shopping company contacts you with an assignment or a question.

Don't let phone messages and email pile up.

Do be willing to take on a last minute assignment, or go a little out of your way to do a shop when the mystery shopping company is in a crunch.

Don't cause a crunch by canceling at the last minute or failing to do a shop you accepted.

Do turn in complete reports and any receipts or other required documentation.

Don't submit incomplete information that causes the company to have to call you.

And always remember to be polite and considerate. The people at mystery shopping companies are just that—*people*. They have good days and bad days, and they have to deal with stress, just like you. Be courteous and cooperative when you work with them and help make their jobs a little easier. They will remember you as a shopper with whom they enjoy working.

Other Jobs for Mystery Shoppers

There are several other jobs that may appeal to mystery shoppers. Once you contract with mystery shopping companies, you may be offered opportunities to do other kinds of work for them.

In the Mystery Shopping Directory in Appendix A of this book you will find several companies that also hire contractors for these types of jobs as well as mystery shopping

Telephone Surveys

As a mystery shopper, you may perform mystery shops by telephone—that is, making a call to a catalog order desk or a customer service department, or calling a restaurant before your visit. Telephone surveys are different. A survey involves calling your client's customers or prospective customers and asking questions. This is not telemarketing, and telephone surveyers aren't selling anything.

Have you ever gotten a call from someone who wanted to know your opinion on something, or your experience with a company or product? That's a telephone survey.

Telephone surveys are often conducted with a client's customers, to get their opinions about the company. For example, after having a garage door opener installed, the company contacted me to make sure that the installer had been here on time, that he had done a good job, that the opener was working properly, that he had cleaned up after the job, etc. They wanted to be sure that the installer was doing a good job, and to take care of any problems if I wasn't satisfied.

You have been on the receiving end of telephone surveys, so you know how they work. When you perform a telephone survey, the questions you ask will be based on the client's information needs. You will be given a list of questions to ask, and the names and phone numbers of the people you are to call.

Telephone survey work may be available at call centers, or you may be able to get work which you can do from your own home.

Focus Groups

Focus groups are groups of people (anywhere from two or three people to more than 100) who answer questions or discuss issues relating to the client's business. Usually, group participants don't know who the client is. They are told only that someone wants their opinions about (for example) shopping for children's clothes. The group might include people who are current customers of the client, those who do business with their competitors, or a mixture. Focus groups are also used to gauge public opinion on political and social issues and many other purposes.

When a large group is used, members of the focus group may each fill out a questionnaire and there may be little or no discussion. I have been a participant in focus groups for local radio stations where there are 100 or more participants. Each person is given a form with a number scale, and the market researchers play a few seconds from each of 600 songs. Participants give their opinions on the songs by circling the corresponding number on the form (e.g., don't like, a favorite, etc.).

Many focus groups have six to twelve participants, and the members of the group talk about a issue. The discussion is usually recorded on video or audio tape, but the taping is done discreetly so it does not inhibit discussion.

Participants in focus groups are usually paid a fee ranging from $10 or $20 to $100 or more. Many people enjoy being a part of a focus group not only because of the money, but because they like having their opinions heard.

If you would like to be a participant in focus groups, contact some market research companies in your area and ask if you might qualify for any focus groups. Start by checking with companies located in your local shopping mall. Some companies will accept participants this way, others take a position of "don't call us, we'll call you." Watch Help Wanted ads in your local newspaper. There are sometimes ads under General or Part Time headings for people to participate in market research studies and focus groups.

Mock Juries

These are also called *shadow juries* and by other names. Law firms use mock juries to test how the actual jury in a trial might respond to certain information. By getting a group of people with characteristics similar to the actual jury, they can judge how a trial is proceeding, or how to introduce certain facts of the case. The mock jury may meet one or two days (often over a weekend), or they may meet every day of an ongoing trial. Pay is often $100 - $250 per day (or more) plus meals and some expenses. Certainly more than you get for being a real juror!

Watch your local newspaper's help wanted ads in the General or Part Time classifications for opportunities to participate in a mock jury.

Merchandising

Some companies that hire mystery shoppers also hire merchandisers, and you may get both types of assignments from them.

What is merchandising? When you get one of these assignments, you will typically be working for a manufacturer rather than the retailer. It may involve going to a store and checking inventory to see if stock is low and the store needs to place an order for more of the manufacturer's goods. You may be asked to deliver an order and put it on the shelves. Sometimes you will set up a display and stock it. Or, just check a display and make sure it is neat and organized.

You may be asked to verify how merchandise is priced and displayed, including signage and what other products are nearby. Unlike when you are mystery shopping, you will identify yourself to store personnel and let them know why you are there. You may need to get a manager's signature to authorize an order, or to verify that you were in the store.

Merchandisers are often paid by the hour, but may be paid by the job. Some jobs will include a reimbursement for mileage. If you are offered an assignment as a merchandiser, you will be told what you are to do and how much you will be paid. Just as with the mystery shopping assignments, you are free to accept or reject any of these jobs.

Pricing Audits

When performing pricing audits you enter a business and note the prices for certain items. This might involve going in to a fast food restaurant and getting prices for several menu items, or doing a detailed survey of prices in a grocery store.

These audits are usually done on behalf of a competitor of the business you are auditing so, as with mystery shopping, you don't announce your presence and gather your information discreetly.

Market Research

Many of the companies which do mystery shopping also do other types of market research, so you may be offered opportunities to conduct surveys as a market researcher or to get paid for giving your opinions by participating in market research studies.

This might include interviewing people over the phone or in person (such as those folks with the clipboards at your local mall), doing price comparisons, participating in taste tests or product trials, etc.

You may be asked to conduct exit interviews. This usually involves standing outside a business and asking questions of customers as they leave. You conduct these interviews with the knowledge of the manager—nothing mysterious here. Pay can be by the hour or by the completed survey.

On the Internet there are sites which recruit participants in market research studies or to complete surveys, etc. Some pay in cash, while others award "points" which can be redeemed for merchandise. Before spending a lot of time filling out surveys, make sure you know exactly what you receive in return.

Should You Start Your Own Mystery Shopping Company?

After you've been mystery shopping for a while, you may decide that you want to start a mystery shopping business of your own. One obvious advantage is that you may be able to make more money in a business of your own than when you are shopping as a contractor for someone else. Of course, like any other business, starting a mystery shopping company comes with cost and risk.

The things you enjoy about mystery shopping can make you a good candidate to start your own mystery shopping business. The best mystery shoppers are those who value excellent customer service and are passionate about providing information that helps businesses improve and become more successful.

On the other hand, there is a big difference between doing mystery shops and running a mystery shopping company. As the business owner you are responsible for selling your service to clients, hiring and managing shoppers, making sure reports are all completed on time, reviewing and editing the reports, submitting data to clients, invoicing clients, paying shoppers and more. You may find that you miss the days of being "just a shopper."

Many of today's successful mystery shopping companies were started by people just like you. After you've weighed all the pros and cons, you may decide that mystery shopping is the business for you. If so, here are some tips to get started.

It helps if you have experience in a customer service industry, such as retail or hospitality. Not only will you know what is required to deliver great service in those industries, you probably have contacts you can use to get your first clients. Perhaps a company you used to work for would like to hire you to mystery shop them.

General business and management experience is useful. As the business owner, you will have to manage staff, oversee collections and financial issues, train new shoppers, and use other skills you honed as a supervisor or manager.

Make sure you didn't sign a non-compete agreement with any of the mystery shopping companies you've worked for. This type of agreement (or it may be a clause in your independent contractor agreement) says that you can not start your own mystery shopping company while you are working for them, and often for a period of one year after you no longer work for them.

If you have signed any non-compete agreements, immediately ask those companies to remove you from their shopper data bases. You would be wise to consult an attorney regarding when you may start your own business after giving such notice.

Don't violate the confidentiality agreements you signed with other mystery shopping companies by copying their report forms, applications, contracts, training manuals, web sites or other proprietary information.

Your independent contractor agreements may prohibit you from approaching companies you mystery shopped as a contractor. When in doubt, consult with an attorney.

You can begin your business part time, but make sure you are available to clients when they need you. Check messages frequently, or use a voice mail system that pages you when messages are received, so you can respond quickly to calls.

Because you will be going to your clients, and your clients won't be coming to you, you can start the business from your home. You will want a separate phone line to use for business, and you may want an address other than your home address to use for business. It is inexpensive to rent a post office box or private mail box.

Many executive suites have business identity programs. These programs allow you to use their mailing address and provide access to other services. You can have your phone line directed to them so your phone is always answered during business hours, they often have secretarial and administrative services available, and they have offices and conference rooms which you can rent as needed.

Don't try to be all things to all people. Your business may expand to cover all types of evaluations, but at the beginning you may want to specialize in an industry where you have experience.

Pricing can be tricky. Your service doesn't have to be the cheapest to get customers. In fact, setting prices too low can cost you customers. If you don't value your service, why should potential customers?

Many new business owners make the mistake of underpricing because they don't consider all the costs of doing business. Remember that it's not just the direct costs and your time to do a shop. You have overhead expenses (such as rent, phone lines, a web site, etc.), marketing expenses, and as you grow you will have to pay shoppers, schedulers and editors, and other staff.

Get help. General business assistance is available from the Small Business Administration and other agencies. They can help you with start up issues, marketing and more.

Consult with an attorney when drafting legal documents such as client contracts, independent contractor agreements, etc.

Build a network of shoppers right from the start, or work with someone (such as a scheduler) who already has a network. You can't do every shop yourself, both because you won't have the time to do all of the shops plus everything else you have to do, and because your clients want observations by people other than you. Most clients don't want the same shopper evaluating the business any more often than every three months.

For industry assistance, one of your first steps should be to join the Mystery Shopping Providers Association <http://www.mysteryshop.org>. You will get to know the people at many other mystery shopping companies, and you will have the opportunity to learn from their experience. Your "competition" may be your greatest asset in starting your new business.

**Many mystery shopping companies
(local, regional, national and international)
are members of the
Mystery Shopping Providers Association.
Visit their web site at
http://www.mysteryshop.org/
for job postings, a message board, links to
member companies' web sites and more.**

What Are You Waiting For?

You now have the information you need to get started as a mystery shopper. Decide right now what your next step is, and get started today.

The Action Plan on page 121 gives you a step-by-step plan to get started. Follow the plan and you will be on your way to being a professional shopper. It may take several weeks to get your first assignment, so get started right away.

Don't wait—do it now! The sooner you start, the sooner you will start earning money, along with free food, services, and merchandise.

For updates to this book and additional information on mystery shopping, visit http://www.IdeaLady.com/.

Send your comments on mystery shopping, this book, and your experiences with mystery shopping companies to me at the address below. I always enjoy hearing from fellow shoppers.

Happy shopping!

Cathy Stucker
4646 Highway 6, PMB#123
Sugar Land, Texas 77478

email: cathy@idealady.com

Action Plan

Here is your step-by-step plan to getting paid to shop and eat as a mystery shopper. Start now and be on your way to becoming a professional shopper!

☐ Write your one-page resume and one-page letter of interest. (See page 48.)

☐ Identify up to ten zip codes where you are willing to shop. (See pages 49 - 50.)

☐ Compose short paragraphs (about 35 - 100 words each) on the following subjects:
- An example of good customer service;
- An example of poor customer service; and
- Why you want to be a mystery shopper/ why you would make a good shopper.

It's helpful to have these on hand, as many applications will ask for them, both when applying online and filling out paper applications. Write them once, then copy when completing applications. (See Applying Online on page 44.)

☐ Choose local and national companies to apply to.(See Appendix A and Appendix B.)

☐ Submit applications online, or mail resumes and letters of interest. (Don't forget to include a self-addressed, stamped envelope with each mailed resume.)

☐ Follow up promptly when contacted by a mystery shopping company. Complete and return applications, call as directed to confirm assignments, complete and return reports by the deadlines, etc.

☐ Continue locating and applying to additional companies to receive more work.

☐ Each step of the way, be professional, be ethical, and have fun!

Appendix A: Mystery Shopping Directory

This section includes contact information for companies that hire mystery shoppers, including mystery shopping companies, schedulers and businesses that hire mystery shoppers directly. These companies have sites on the Internet, and most of them allow you to make your application online. In fact, most prefer that you apply online.

To jump start your mystery shopping career, sit at the computer with this list and start making applications to the companies that most interest you. You won't always know which companies need shoppers in your area, and companies' needs change over time. To get started quickly and make yourself eligible for more assignments, apply to many companies. Start out by applying to at least 20 companies, and apply to a few more from time to time. If you've done the preparation recommended in the Action Plan on page 121, you should be able to submit 20, 30 or more applications in a single evening at the computer.

Pay attention to the information given with each listing. If a company wants experienced shoppers, don't apply until you have experience. If they have any requirement you don't meet, don't waste your time and theirs by submitting an application.

The list includes phone numbers for many companies, but **do not call unless the company has indicated you may**. Many of these companies have a small staff dealing with hundreds or thousands of shops and shoppers at a time. They don't have time to chat. The phone numbers are included here for easy reference if you need to reach a company you are working with.

This list is presented for your information, and the inclusion of a company on this list does not imply a recommendation of that company.

We have attempted to include only companies which do not require an application fee or other charges for accepting you as a mystery shopper, or at least to note any charges we were told about.

This company list was current as we went to press in March, 2002; however, the business changes rapidly, so expect that some companies will change their hiring practices and others will change name, web site or physical address, or go out of business.

If you are unable to reach a company's web site through the URL listed here, there are several possible reasons. It may be that the web site is temporarily unavailable, so try it again later. The URL may have changed, so you might try doing a search for the company name at Google.com or other search engines. Of course, it is also possible that the company is no longer in business or they are doing business under another name.

If you've gone through this list and still want more, there are many other companies that do mystery shopping. Review the information on How to Find More Companies in Appendix B to locate additional mystery shopping companies (including companies operating locally).

Mystery Shopping Companies

A & M Business Services
P.O. Box 34073
Pensacola, FL 32507
850-492-7467
850-492-7865 fax
http://www.ambussvcs.com/
National company. They specialize in the hospitality industry.
Date Applied: _____

A Closer Look
P.O. Box 920760
Norcross, GA 30010-0760
770-446-0590
770-448-2091 fax
http://www.a-closer-look.com/
National company.
Date Applied: _____

ACRA, Inc.
P.O. Box 431
Mantua, NJ 08051
http://www.secretshopacra.com/
U.S./Canada
Date Applied: _____

A Customer's Point of View
9442 S. Main Street, Suite 119A
Jonesboro, GA 30236
770-477-1719
770-477-7920 fax
http://www.acpview.com/
National company.
Date Applied: _____

Amusement Advantage
Wheat Ridge, CO
800-362-9946
303-234-9946 fax
http://www.amusementadvantage.com/
Amusement Advantage evaluates amusement parks,
zoos, museums, arcades and other attractions.
Date Applied: _____

Anonymous Insights, Inc.
7438 Sawmill Road, PMB# 421
Columbus, OH 43235
http://www.a-insights.com/
National company.
Date Applied: _____

Ath Power Consulting
Andover, MA
877-977-6937
http://www.athpower.com/what/2_3_1_become.html
National company. They specialize in financial
services and retail. The URL listed goes directly to
their mystery shopper information page. Or, you can,
go to the home page at http://www.athpower.com/ and
follow the Mystery Shopping link.
Date Applied: _____

Bare Associates International
3251 Old Lee Highway, Suite 209
Fairfax, VA 22030-1504
800-296-6699
703-591-6583 fax
http://www.baiservices.com/
Worldwide. Bare Associates shops hotels, restaurants, bars, retail, health clubs, golf courses, etc. Many of their assignments require narrative reports. They also have assignments involving customer exit interviews, where you survey customers as they exit a business.
Date Applied: _____

BestMark
4915 West 35th Street, Suite 206
St. Louis Park, MN 55416
800-514-8378
952-922-0237 fax
http://www.bestmark.com/
U.S./Canada/Puerto Rico. BestMark shops a wide variety of industries, including restaurants, retail stores, casinos, banks, travel and more. Shoppers must be 21 years of age or older, have reliable transportation, have good written communication skills, and must have full Internet access at home or at work.
Date Applied: _____

Beyond Hello Inc.
P.O. Box 5240
Madison, WI 53705
800-321-2588
800-868-5203
http://www.beyondhello.com/
U.S./Canada/Others.
Date Applied: _____

BMA Mystery Shopping
P.O. Box 600
Oaks, PA 19456
610-933-6061
610-933-6071 fax
http://www.mystery-shopping.com/
U.S./Canada/Puerto Rico/Europe.
Date Applied: _____

Brand Marketing International
Mystery Shopper, USA
Sarasota, FL
http://www.bmiltd.com/
International. Their focus is retail, and they want shoppers who have experience in mystery shopping or consumer research. Retail experience is a plus.
Date Applied: _____

Business Evaluation Services
2920 F Street, #E-15
Bakersfield, CA 93301
888-300-8292
661-631-1685 fax
http://www.mysteryshopperservices.com/
National company.
Date Applied: _____

The Business Research Lab
http://www.busreslab.com/
This company says they do mystery shopping, online
mystery shopping and survey panels.
Date Applied: _____

Byer's Choice, Inc.
224 Wexham Drive
Reading, PA 19607
610-796-7211
610-796-7229 fax
http://byerschoiceinc.com/
Their clients are primarily in the Northeast and Mid-
Atlantic areas, but they are expanding to other areas.
Date Applied: _____

Campbell, Edgar Inc.
4388 - 49th Street
Delta, BC Canada V4K 2S7
604-946-8535
604-946-2384 fax
http://www.retailmysteryshoppers.com/
U.S./Canada.
Date Applied: _____

Capstone Research
Fairfield, NJ
973-575-6161
http://www.capstoneresearch.com/
National company.
Date Applied: _____

Certified Reports, Inc. & Certified Marketing Services
7 Hudson Street
Kinderhook, NY 12106
518-758-6400
518-758-6451 fax
http://www.certifiedreports.com/
http://www.certifiedmarketingservices.com/
National company. They mystery shop theatres and a
variety of retailers. They also do retail merchandising
and theatre audits and surveys. You can apply online
by following the links for Fieldworker Access.
Date Applied: _____

CheckMark, Inc.
4013 Bach-Buxton Road
Batavia, OH 45103
http://www.checkmarkinc.com/
U.S./Canada/Puerto Rico.
Date Applied: _____

Check Up Marketing
5109 Holly Ridge Drive, Suite 210
Raleigh, North Carolina 27612
919-782-7581
919-782-2329 fax
http://www.checkupmarketing.com
National company.
Date Applied: _____

Cirrus Marketing Consultants
9852 W. Katella Avenue, #207
Anaheim, CA 92804
714-899-7600
714-899-7604 fax
http://www.cirrusmktg.com/
National company.
Date Applied: _____

Courtesy Counts
7825 Tuckerman Lane, Suite 213
Potomac, MD 20854
301-299-5400
301-299-7008 fax
http://www.courtesycounts.com/
Nationalcompany.
Date Applied: _____

Customer 1st
225 Commerce Place
Greensboro, NC 27401
336-378-6300
336-378-6466 fax
http://www.customer-1st.com/
National company.
Date Applied: _____

Customer Perspectives
213 West River Road
Hooksett, NH 03106-2628
603-647-1300
603-647-0900 fax
http://www.customerperspectives.com/
National company. They shop restaurants,
department and specialty stores and banks. Web site
includes a list of "Hot Spots" where shoppers are
needed immediately.
Date Applied: _____

Data Quest Investigations/Service Quest
667 Boylston Street, Suite 200
Boston, MA 02116
617-437-0030
617-437-0034
http://www.dataquestonline.com/
National company. Applications for mystery shoppers and other available positions are on the web site. Access by following the "Employment Opportunities" link.
Date Applied: _____

David Sparks & Associates
107 Clemson Street
Clemson, SC 29631
864-654-7571
864-654-3229 fax
http://www.sparksresearch.com/
National company.
Date Applied: _____

DSG Associates, Inc.
2110 East First Street, Suite 106
Santa Ana, CA 92705-4019
714-835-3020
714-835-6506 fax
http://www.dsgai.com/
National company.
Date Applied: _____

Elrick & Lavidge
770-621-7600
http://www.elavidge.com/msapplication.htm
National company.
Date Applied: _____

Employee Evaluators
1710 Manor Hill Road
Findlay, OH 45840
http://www.mysteryshops.com/
National company.
Date Applied: _____

Eye on Retail
468 Morden Road
Oakville, Ontario Canada L6K 3W4
http://www.shopper.eyeonretail.com/
Canada. Application and instructions are at the web site.
Date Applied: _____

Feedback Plus
5580 Peterson Lane, Suite 120 LB19
Dallas, TX 75240-5157
972-661-8989
http://www.gofeedback.com/
U.S./Canada/Puerto Rico.
Date Applied: _____

Golden Resources
P.O. Box 71314
Marietta, GA 30007-1314
http://members.aol.com/cgr315/
National company. You can apply online via email, or send a self-addressed, stamped envelope for an application. You may also print the online application and mail it to them.
Date Applied: _____

Green & Associates Mystery Shoppers
P.O. Box 9869
College Station, TX 77845
800-677-2260
979-693-7904 fax
http://www.greenandassociates.com/
National company. They specialize in the hospitality industry.
Date Applied: _____

Greet America
http://www.ga-mysteryshopper.com/
U.S. and Canada. Experience is required, and you must have dependable transportation.
Date Applied: _____

Hilli Dunlap Enterprises, Inc.
P.O. Box 15487
North Hollywood, CA 91615-9774
818-760-7688
http://www.dunlapenterprises.com/
U.S. and Mexico.
Date Applied: _____

Hindsight, Inc.
1762 Windward Way
Sanibel, FL 33957
954-757-9835
253-595-6704 fax
http://www.hndsight.com/
U.S./Canada/Mexico.
Date Applied: _____

Howard Services/Service Sleuths
Franklin Office Park
38 Pond Street, Suite 104
Franklin, MA 02038
508-520-1500
http://www.servicesleuths.com/
National company, with most clients in the New
England and Mid-Atlantic states.
Date Applied: _____

HR and Associates, Inc.
223 Burlington Ave.
Clarendon Hills, IL 60514-1168
630-789-0444
630-323-4066 fax
http://www.hrandassociates.com/
International company.
Date Applied: _____

ICC Decision Services
P.O. Box 188
Wayne, NJ 07474
973-890-8611
973-890-8615 fax
http://www.iccds.com/rep_home.html
National company. They hire for mystery shopping, in-store demonstrations, merchandising and customer interviews.
Date Applied: _____

Infotel, Inc.
3190 South Bascom Avenue
Suite 100
San Jose, CA 95124
800-876-1110 Ext. 34
800-882-1284 fax
http://www.infotelinc.com/
U.S./Canada
Date Applied: _____

IntelliShop
801 W. South Boundary
Suite D
Perrysburg, OH 43551
419-872-5103
419-872-5104 fax
http://www.intelli-shop.com/
National company.
Date Applied: _____

Investigative Marketing Services
Suite 1420, 840-7 Ave. SW
Sandman Office Tower
Calgary, Alberta, Canada T2P 3G2
403-217-8333
403-217-4875 fax
http://www.investigativemarketing.com/
U.S./Canada/Phillipines/Australia/U.K. This company also helps non-profit groups with fundraising. The members perform mystery shops with the proceeds going to support the non-profit organization.
Date Applied: _____

Jack in the Box
Jack's Mystery Guest
http://www.jacksguest.com/
15 states. Jack in the Box hires shoppers to work 5 - 12 hours a week for up to 5 or 6 months. There is paid training, then shoppers receive assignments covering a variety of hours, including nights and weekends. If you are interested in being contacted when they are hiring in your area, fill out the form at the web site.
Date Applied: ＿＿＿＿＿＿＿

Jancyn
P.O. Box 26934
San Jose, CA 95159
408-267-2600
408-267-2602 fax
http://www.jancyn.com/
National company. Jancyn shops retail, restaurants, entertainment and rental housing. Shoppers are paid using PayPal.
Date Applied: ＿＿＿＿＿＿＿

J. M. Ridgway Company, Inc.
1066 Saratoga Ave., Suite 120
San Jose, CA 95129-3401
800-367-7434
408-615-6763 fax
http://www.jmridgway.com/
National company.
Date Applied: ＿＿＿＿＿＿＿

Loews Theatres
800-246-3519/212-833-6653
http://www.loewscineplex.com/mystery/
National movie theater chain. The Loews Theatre chain, which includes Loews, Magic Johnson and Cineplex Odeon Theatres, recruits their own mystery shoppers. You pay a $50 fee to join The Mystery Shopper Club. In return, you receive eight movie tickets and $40 worth of concessions coupons. You choose the theater you will visit when you enroll. The evaluation you have to complete is a simple yes/no form, and no written narrative is required. Get full information about the program and learn how to apply by going to their web site, or by calling either of the numbers listed above.
Date Applied: _____

Maritz Research
1355 North Highway Drive
Fenton, St. Louis County, MO 63099
636-827-8532
636-827-8605 fax
http://www.virtuoso.maritzresearch.com/
http://www.maritzresearch.com/
U.S./U.K. To become a "virtual customer," you can fill out the online application, or call 800-782-4299 in the U.S. or 01628 895543 in the U.K. If accepted, you will work for Maritz as an employee, not as a contractor.
Date Applied: _____

Marketing Systems Unlimited Corp.
1519 South Gilbert Street
Iowa City, IA 52240
319-338-3773
319-338-0513 fax
http://www.msultd.com/
National company. They hire for full and part time.
Date Applied: _____

Mars Research
Multiple Locations
954-755-2805
954-755-3061fax
http://www.marsresearch.com/
National company. Follow the links on their web site to Employment or Participateto be considered for mystery shopping assignments or participation in focus groups, taste tests, music surveys, etc.
Date Applied: _____

Michelson & Associates, Inc.
1900 The Exchange, Suite 360
Atlanta, GA 30339
770-955-5400
770-955-5040 fax
http://www.michelson.com/mystery/
U.S./Canada/Puerto Rico. You can apply online at their web site or you can print out the application and fax or mail it to them.
Date Applied: _____

MS Surveys
Brentwood, CA
888-222-8301
888-222-8302 fax
http://www.mercsurveys.com/
U.S./U.K. Shops include golf, dining, entertainment and hotel/motel.
Date Applied: _____

Mystery Shoppers, Inc.
TrendSource, Inc.
111 Elm Street, Suite 100
San Diego, CA 92101
619-239-2543
619-239-2525 fax
http://www.mysteryshoppersinc.com/
U.S./Canada/Puerto   Rico/Jamaica/Guam/Virgin Islands. They shop restaurants, retail, financial services, hotels and resorts, automotive services and many more.
Date Applied: _____

National Shopping Service
Roseville, CA
916-781-6776
916-781-6621 fax
http://www.nssmysteryshoppers.com/
U.S./Europe.
Date Applied: _____

National Shopping Service Network
303-451-0325
http://www.mysteryshopper.net/
U.S./Canada/UK.
Date Applied: _____

Nationwide Integrity Services
12930 Chippewa Road, Suite 2
Cleveland, OH 44141
440-838-8300
440-838-0442 fax
http://www.nationwideintegrity.com/
National company. They are looking for experienced shoppers. Nationwide Integrity shops retail, convenience stores, gas stations, restaurants and more.
Date Applied: _____

Person to Person Quality
625 N. Washington St., Suite 303
Alexandria, VA 22314
703-836-1517
703-836-1895 fax
http://www.persontopersonquality.com/
National company. Their emphasis is on shopping banks, mortgage companies, and insurers. They also do merchandising.
Date Applied: _____

Pinkerton Field Research Services
13950 Ballantine Corporate Place, Suite 300
Charlotte, NC 28277
800-553-9807
888-343-2652 fax
http://www.pktnshop.com/
International company.
Date Applied: _____

Prince Market Research, Inc.
2323 Hillsboro Road
Nashville, TN 37212
615-292-4860
http://www.pmresearch.com/
National company. They hire contractors for their
"virtual call center" to contact customers by telephone
and interview them. It does not involve selling. For
information, click on "Employment" from main web
page.
Date Applied: _____

Professional Review & Operational Shoppers, Inc.
3885 20th Street
Vero Beach, FL 32960
800-741-7758
http://www.proreview.com/
Client base concentrated in 16 states in the east and
southeast areas of the U.S. Specializes in financial
institutions.
Date Applied: _____

Pulseback, Inc.
67 Union Street
P.O. Box 829
Manchester, VT 05254
802-362-0900
802-362-0977 fax
http://www.pulseback.com/
National company.
Date Applied: _____

Quality Assessments Mystery Shopper
P.O. Box 90547
Austin, TX 78709
800-580-2500
http://www.qams.com/
National company.
Date Applied: _____

Quality Check
717-352-9536
717-352-9629 fax
http://undercovershoppers.com/
National company. They shop restaurants, retail, movie theaters, automotive, casinos, travel and more. The web site includes application instructions.
Date Applied: _____

Quality Consultants, Inc.
P.O. Box 454
East Greenwich, RI 02818
401-647-2828
401-647-2835 fax
http://www.qualconsultant.com/
U.S./Canada.
Date Applied: _____

Quality Marketing, Inc.
P.O. Box 746
High Point, NC 27261
1-888-569-7467
http://www.quality-marketing.com/
National company.
Date Applied: _____

Quality Works Associates
282 Moody Street, Suite 206
Waltham, MA 02453
781-398-1678
781-398-1679 fax
http://www.qualityworks.com/myshop.htm
National company.
Date Applied: _____

The Quest for Best
P.O. Box 280933
Memphis, TN 38134
800-263-5202
901-377-1349 fax
http://www.questforbest.com/
National company with clients in over 40 states, with the majority in the midwest and southwest. The web site says shoppers need to have an automobile and a stopwatch.
Date Applied: _____

Retail Biz
5322 222nd Ave. NE
Redmond, WA 98053-8247
425-875-6240
425-836-9149 fax
http://www.retailbiz.com/jobs.html
U.S. and Canada. Shoppers must have a vehicle and drivers license.
Date Applied: _____

Rickie Kruh Research & Marketing Group
171 Somervelle St., Suite 409
Alexandria, VA 22304
http://www.rkrmg.com/
National company. You can apply by emailing your name and contact information to rkrmg@aol.com.
Date Applied: _____

Ritter and Associates, Inc.
4222 Airport Hwy., Suite #5
Toledo, OH 43615
Attn: Dennis Richard
419-381-2270
http://www.ritterandassociates.com/
National company. They prefer to work with shoppers who want responsibility for a geographic area, (e.g., a state). Apply online or print and mail the application.
Date Applied: _____

Rocky Mountain Merchandising & Research
1742 E. Holladay Blvd.
Salt Lake City, UT 84124
801-274-0220
801-274-8066 fax
http://www.rockymm.com/
Operates in many western states (see map at web site). They do mystery shopping, merchandising, audits, in-store demos and more.
Date Applied: _____

Second to None
3045 Miller Road
Ann Arbor, MI 48103
http://www.second-to-none.com/
U.S./Canada/Mexico/Virgin Islands/Other. They shop a wide variety of businesses, including restaurants, retail, financial services institutions, etc.
Date Applied: _____

Secret ShopNET
Calgary, Alberta Canada
http://www.secretshopnet.com/
U.S./Canada. Their clients include gas stations, fast food, retail, etc.
Date Applied: _____

The Secret Shopper Company
Atlanta, GA
678-382-9999
http://www.secretshoppercompany.com/
U.S./Canada/Virgin Islands/Puerto Rico/Dominican Republic.
Date Applied: _____

Secret Shopping Services
35400 26th Place S.
Federal Way, WA 98003
253-661-2734
888-203-4419 fax
http://www.secretshoppingservices.com/
National company.
Date Applied: _____

Sensors Quality Management
220 Duncan Mill Road, Suite 212
Toronto, Ontario Canada M3B 3J5
416-444-4491
416-444-2422 fax
http://www.sqm.ca/
U.S./Canada/Mexico.
Date Applied: _____

Service Advantage International
42207 East Ann Arbor Road
Plymouth, MI 48170
734-453-4750
734-453-4790 fax
http://www.servad.com/
International company.
Date Applied: _____

Service Check
P.O. Box 4124
Redondo Beach, CA 90277-1747
310-763-8340
310-763-8355
http://www.servicecheck.com
National company. The web site indicates that they
are planning to expand to other English-speaking
countries, including Canada and the United Kingdom.
Date Applied: _____

Service Evaluation Concepts
55 East Ames Court
Planview, NY 11803
516-576-1188
516-576-1195 fax
http://www.serviceevaluation.com/
U.S./Canada.
Date Applied: _____

Service Excellence Group
St. Louis, MO
314-878-9189
314-878-1818 fax
http://serviceexcellencegroup.com/
National company.
Date Applied: _____

Service Excellence Group/Customer Service Experts
130 Holiday Court, Suite 104
Annapolis, MD 21401
888-770-7625
http://www.customerserviceexperts.com/
National company. All of their assignments require at least a one-page narrative, so they require a writing sample from applicants.
Date Applied: _____

Service Impressions
P.O. Box 332
Lafayette, CA 94549
925-299-0877
http://www.serviceimpressions.com/
U.S./Canada.
Date Applied: _____

Service Performance Group, Inc.
180 Detroit Street, Suite B
Cary, IL 60013
847-516-8424
847-516-9315 fax
http://www.serviceperformancegrp.com/
U.S. and Canada.
Date Applied: _____

ServiceTRAC, Inc.
1525 N. Granite Reef Road, Suite 11
Scottsdale, AZ 85257
480-941-3121
480-941-5246 fax
http://www.servicetrac.com/
National company. They shop senior housing and retirement facilities, restaurants, hotels, stores, casinos and other industries.
Date Applied: _____

Ser-View
Carlson Center
Two Carlson Parkway, Suite 350
Plymouth, MN 55447
800-336-2691
763-249-2478 fax
http://www.ser-view.com/
National company.
Date Applied: _____

SG Marketing Group
P.O. Box 773
Arnold, CA 95223
209-795-0830
209-795-5829 fax
http://www.sgmarketing.com/
U.S./Canada. Request an application online.
Date Applied: _____

The Shadow Agency/Shadow Shopper
229 Circleview Drive South
Hurst, TX 76054
817-268-3338
817-282-3070 fax
http://www.shadowagency.com/
National company. They conduct audio and video mystery shops nationally. There isn't an application at the web site, but they are preparing to launch a site at http://www.shadowshopper.com/ where shoppers can register (for a fee) and be included in a data base to receive notices of assignments available from participating companies and have access to other shopping resources.
Date Applied: _____

Shoney's Restaurants
P.O. Box 1260
Nashville, TN 37202
615-231-2281 / 877-835-5746
615-231-2604 fax
http://www.shoneysrestaurants.com/mystery_shoppe r_application.htm
Shoney's Restaurants include Shoney's and Captain D's. You choose a location and they will reimburse you for meals in exchange for completing evaluation forms. Apply online or call 1-877-835-5227.
Date Applied: _____

Shop'n Chek Worldwide.
Post Office Box 740045
Atlanta, GA 30374-0045
Attn: Field Personnel
http://www.shopnchek.com/shopper.html
U.S./Canada/Puerto Rico/Guam. The web site has instructions for applying online or via postal mail.
Date Applied: _____

Shoppers' Critique International
636 Florida Central Parkway
Longwood, FL 32750
407-834-4001
407-834-2328 fax
http://www.shopperscritique.com/
Web site says they shop the U.S. and "the World". Industries shopped include restaurants, retail, theme parks, automotive, hotels and resorts, and new home sales.
Date Applied: _____

Shoppers' View
800-264-5677
616-447-1236 fax
http://www.shoppersview.com/
National company.
Date Applied: _____

Sights on Service, Inc.
Minneapolis, MN
http://www.mysteryshop.com/
http://www.secretshop.com/
http://www.secretshopper.com/
National company. They shop restaurants, auto service providers, grocery stores and more.
Date Applied: _____

Sinclair Service Assessments, Inc.
900 Isom, Suite 110
San Antonio, TX 78216-4116
http://www.ssanet.com/
International.
Date Applied: _____

Sparagowski & Associates
5855 Monroe Street
Sylvania, OH 43560
419-885-2591
419-882-7426 fax
http://www.sparagowski.com/
National company. They hire full time "inspectors" (preferably couples) who are responsible for an assigned territory. Get full information at the web site.
Date Applied: _____

Speedmark
719 Sawdust Road, Suite 300
The Woodlands, TX 77380
281-363-3945
http://www.speedmarkweb.com/
National company. Speedmark hires contractors for mystery shopping, data collection and merchandising. These and other positions are posted at the web site.
Date Applied: _____

Spot Checks
P.O. Box 13462
LaJolla, CA 92039-3462
858-693-6978
http://www.spotchecks.com/
National company.
Date Applied: _____

Tenox Appraisal Services
2140 Winston Park Drive
Unit #31
Oakville, Ontario, Canada L6H 5V5
905-829-9548
905-829-3202 fax
http://www.weshop4u.com/
Canada.
Date Applied: _____

TES/RapidChek
3619 Motor Ave., Suite 300
Los Angeles, CA 90034
310-840-5800
800-443-6093 fax
http://www.rapidchek.com/
U.S./Puerto Rico/Canada. Their focus is movie theaters, and they also do retail shops. In addition to mystery shopping movie theaters, they collect box office gross information, view previews, and evaluate the performance of sneak previews.
Date Applied: _____

Texas Shoppers Network
908 Town & Country Blvd., Suite 120
Houston, TX 77024
713-984-7631
281-293-9917 fax
http://www.texasshoppersnetwork.com/
National company. The application can be completed online, or you may print it out and fax or mail it.
Date Applied: _____

A Top Shop!
8156-E South Wadsworth Blvd., Suite 220
Littleton, CO 80128
720-283-8377
720-283-8366 fax
http://www.atopshop.com/
National company.
Date Applied: _____

Schedulers

Kern Scheduling Services
Lorri Kern
Lakeside, CA
Email: KSSLorri@aol.com
http://www.sassieshop.com/kern
U.S./Canada/Puerto Rico. Apply at the web site, or send an email with your name, address, telephone numbers, email address, and any other information (e.g., demographics, your experience and where you are willing to shop) that might be helpful in scheduling you for shops.
Date Applied: _____

Palm Scheduling Services
Cheryl Durbin
Whittier, CA
562-944-1313
Email: PSSScheduler1@aol.com
http://www.palmschedulingservices.com/
U.S./Canada. Apply at the web site, or send an email with your name, address, telephone numbers, email address, where you are willing to shop, and any other information that could help in scheduling you for shops
Date Applied: _____

Other Companies

Use these pages to keep track of other mystery shopping companies you've located and applied to.

Company: _____

Address: _____

City/State/Zip: _____

Phone: _____

Fax: _____

Web Site: _____

Notes: _____

Company: _____

Address: _____

City/State/Zip: _____

Phone: _____

Fax: _____

Web Site: _____

Notes: _____

Company: _____

Address: _____

City/State/Zip: _____

Phone: _____

Fax: _____

Web Site: _____

Notes: _____

Company: _____

Address: _____

City/State/Zip: _____

Phone: _____

Fax: _____

Web Site: _____

Notes: _____

Company: _____

Address: _____

City/State/Zip: _____

Phone: _____

Fax: _____

Web Site: _____

Notes: _____

Company: _____

Address: _____

City/State/Zip: _____

Phone: _____

Fax: _____

Web Site: _____

Notes: _____

Company: _____

Address: _____

City/State/Zip: _____

Phone: _____

Fax: _____

Web Site: _____

Notes: _____

Company: _____

Address: _____

City/State/Zip: _____

Phone: _____

Fax: _____

Web Site: _____

Notes: _____

Company: _____

Address: _____

City/State/Zip: _____

Phone: _____

Fax: _____

Web Site: _____

Notes: _____

Company: _____

Address: _____

City/State/Zip: _____

Phone: _____

Fax: _____

Web Site: _____

Notes: _____

Company: _____

Address: _____

City/State/Zip: _____

Phone: _____

Fax: _____

Web Site: _____

Notes: _____

Company: _____

Address: _____

City/State/Zip: _____

Phone: _____

Fax: _____

Web Site: _____

Notes: _____

Company: _____

Address: _____

City/State/Zip: _____

Phone: _____

Fax: _____

Web Site: _____

Notes: _____

Company: _____

Address: _____

City/State/Zip: _____

Phone: _____

Fax: _____

Web Site: _____

Notes: _____

Company: _____

Address: _____

City/State/Zip: _____

Phone: _____

Fax: _____

Web Site: _____

Notes: _____

Company: _____

Address: _____

City/State/Zip: _____

Phone: _____

Fax: _____

Web Site: _____

Notes: _____

Company: _____

Address: _____

City/State/Zip: _____

Phone: _____

Fax: _____

Web Site: _____

Notes: _____

Appendix B: How to Find More Mystery Shopping Companies

The previous section contains contact information for many mystery shopping companies that hire shoppers across the country, or even around the world. There are also mystery shopping companies that only shop in a limited area—perhaps your city or state. In this section, you'll learn how to find those companies, as well as how to find more national and international companies.

To find mystery shopping companies in your area, check the Yellow Pages of your phone directory. If you have separate Yellow Pages directories for consumers and businesses, these companies will be in the business directory. Your phone book won't have a heading for "Mystery Shopping", so try looking under these headings:

Shopping Services - Commercial
Shopping Services-Protective, Price Comparison

You can find mystery shopping leads by talking to other mystery shoppers and exchanging information about shopping. You're saying, "But I don't know any mystery shoppers!" Chances are, you do. It has just never come up before, or you didn't pay attention when they mentioned it. When you are more aware of mystery shopping, suddenly you'll meet other shoppers at parties, your child's play group, all over.

When talking about mystery shopping with others, don't give out proprietary information. Don't talk about fees or specific shops, but it's acceptable to say that you have shopped for ABC Mystery Shoppers and to tell another shopper how to contact them.

You can exchange information with other shoppers by visiting message boards and joining email lists on the Internet. See Appendix C to learn where the message boards and mailing lists are. These services are free.

Watch the Help Wanted ads in your local newspaper. Occasionally, a company needing shoppers in an area will place a classified ad. They usually appear under the General or Part Time headings. You can also find merchandising jobs this way.

Call temporary help agencies and ask if they have a need for contract shoppers. Some of the larger agencies especially will sometimes place shoppers for mystery shopping companies, or mystery shop for their clients. This is an especially good idea if you are looking for other part time or temporary work, too.

Don't forget the warnings on page 53 about scams!

Using the Internet

One of the best resources for locating mystery shopping companies is the Internet. A good place to locate mystery shopping companies and jobs is the Mystery Shopping Providers Association at: http://www.mysteryshop.org/. You can search for jobs in your state, or to find companies by region, industry served or the types of shops they do.

There are lists of mystery shopping companies available for free on several web sites. Remember that the saying, "You get what you pay for," is frequently true. These lists are often out of date and you may spend a lot of time trying to reach companies that no longer exist. Some of the mystery shopping companies they name only shop in a small, local area. If you live in Chicago you don't want to waste your time (and theirs) applying to a company that only shops in Cincinnati.

I contacted companies from one list and found that many of them were market research companies, but they do not mystery shop, have never mystery shopped, and have no future plans to mystery shop. If you send a resume to them, you will either get no response, or they will have to take the time to let you know they don't hire mystery shoppers.

The list of companies in this book will get you off to a good start. If you decide you want to apply to more companies, or different companies, check the MSPA site, look for companies offline using the suggestions earlier in this chapter, or search for companies online using the techniques that follow.

What to Do If You Don't Have Internet Access

Even if you don't have a computer or Internet access at home, you can find companies and apply to them online. Some mystery shopping companies want you to have full time Internet access at home or at work, but most don't care how you get to the Internet, as long as you can get online when you need to contact them, download shop forms and instructions, and submit reports.

Many public libraries and university libraries have Internet access available to the public without charge. Call your local libraries and ask if they have this service available. They may also have free orientation sessions to teach you how to use the computers and find what you are looking for on the Internet. If not, the librarians can assist you in getting started.

Your employer may allow personal use of company computers. Make sure you're not violating company policy before using an employer's equipment or Internet account.

Friends or family members who have computers and Internet accounts might let you use their computers to apply to and keep in touch with mystery shopping companies. This could be a good temporary solution until you get your own computer.

There are businesses that offer computer and Internet access at hourly rates. The cost will eat into your profits, but this is a solution if you don't have any other way.

Remember that many business expenses are tax deductible. That means that you may be able to deduct some or all of the cost of your computer, printer, Internet connection, etc. Consider using some of your mystery shopping income to pay for a new computer and online service.

Searching the Web

Whether you are using your own Internet account, or accessing the Internet through a public terminal or that of a friend, here is what you should do once you are connected to the web:

There are many *search engines* available to help you find what you are looking for. A search engine is like an index to help you find what you're looking for in the vastness of the Internet. A few of the best-known search engines are Yahoo, Google, Alta Vista, and Lycos. The service you are using to connect to the Internet may have a list of search engines with *hotlinks*. When you move the cursor (the little arrow you move around the screen with the mouse) over a hotlink, the arrow will change to a pointing hand. This means that if you click the left mouse button, it will connect you to the site.

If you can't find a list of search engines, your best bet is to go directly to Yahoo. The software you are using (called a *browser*) will have a place on the screen where you can type in the *URL* (address) of the site you want to go to. Usually it is a box near the top of the screen. Key in http://www.yahoo.com/, then press <enter>.

When you get to Yahoo, there will be a box on the screen where you enter the subject of the search. Type in "mystery shopping" then press the <enter> key or click on the <Search> button on the screen. (To click on something on your screen, move the mouse until the cursor is positioned over the thing you want to click on. Then, press the left mouse button.)

The list of entries you get will each have a hotlink which you can click on to visit the site. After visiting the site, click on the <Back> button on the screen until you get back to your list of sites at Yahoo. Then, visit the next site, and so on.

You can run the same search on several other search engines. Each search engine will give you some different results. Try one or more of these:

http://www.google.com/
http://www.altavista.com/
http://www.lycos.com/

Hints for Searching the Web:

For best results when doing your search, search for "mystery shopper" or "mystery shopping". Searching for "mystery shop" will get more results; however, many of the pages you find will have nothing to do with mystery shopping. They will be for mystery bookshops, stores which sell Dungeons and Dragons materials, occult-related sites, etc.

Use quote marks around your search term (e.g., "mystery shopping") to get better results. If you just type the two words, (e.g., mystery shopping) some search engines will give you a list of all the places that use either one of the words, not just the two words used together.

You will find many places offering to sell information about mystery shopping. Like every place else you can buy things, some are legitimate and some are not. Refer to the section on scams on page 53 and consider carefully before sending money.

You will find sites with free lists of mystery shopping companies. I've checked out some of these lists and found some good information, but a lot of listings were out of date, incomplete, or include companies that operate only in a small local or regional area, or that don't do mystery shopping at all (and never have). So don't spend a lot of time or postage applying to lots of companies you found on a "free" list.

Be prepared before going online. Have your information ready to input. Take a little time beforehand to prepare short statements about why you believe you would make a good mystery shopper, as well as examples of good and bad customer service you have received. Several of the online applications ask questions such as these. Keep them fairly short—35 to 100 words, in most cases.

When applying online, use common sense regarding what you disclose. Most of the people you encounter on the Internet are honest, but don't give out any information you wouldn't give someone who called you on the phone until you are certain of who you are dealing with.

Appendix C:
Internet Resources

IdeaLady

http://www.IdeaLady.com/

To keep up with new developments and updates on mystery shopping, be sure to visit the author's web site.

Mystery Shopping Providers Association

http://www.mysteryshop.org/

A great resource for mystery shoppers, mystery shopping companies, and businesses seeking mystery shopping services. Shoppers will find job postings, a message board, and lots of links to mystery shopping companies.

Volition.com

http://www.volition.com/mystery.html

Lots of links to mystery shopping companies, message boards, and other shopper resources. They also have links to information on merchandising and in-store demo jobs. The site includes a message board and they host live chats regularly.

Message Boards

There are message boards, forums and email discussion lists on the Internet where schedulers and mystery shopping companies post leads for mystery shopping and merchandising assignments. You may also be able to exchange information with other shoppers and learn more about mystery shopping.

Instructions for using these resources will be found at the sites listed. You may go to a web site to read or post messages, or some will allow you to have messages delivered directly to you via email.

You will find several message boards, forums and discussion lists by searching for "mystery shopping," "secret shopping," and "merchandising" on these sites:

http://www.delphiforums.com/
http://www.topica.com/
http://www.yahoogroups.com/

Appendix D: Frequently Asked Questions

Here are some of the questions many new shoppers ask about mystery shopping.

What is mystery shopping?

Mystery shoppers go into businesses as customers. They interact with employees, make a purchase and possibly a return, then fill out an evaluation form describing what happened during their visit. Mystery shoppers get paid for providing this service.

What kinds of businesses use mystery shoppers?

Any business which deals with the public may use mystery shoppers—stores, restaurants, banks, hotels, salons, home builders, apartment complexes, gas stations, casinos, auto dealers, auto service centers, movie theaters, health clubs, pet stores, amusement parks, optical providers and more. You can get paid to get your hair cut or your eyes examined, have dinner, go to the bank, have your car worked on or fill up the gas tank, watch a movie, get your dog groomed, and lots of other things you like to (or have to) do.

How much will I earn?

That depends on you. Many shoppers do this in their spare time, and earn $100, $200, or more per month. Some consistently earn more—often a lot more. It is not unusual for a part time or spare time shopper to make $300, $500 or more per month. Some shoppers work for a large number of companies, or are full time with one company, and make their living this way.

There are some mystery shoppers who shop full time and earn a living this way. It's not easy, though, to be a full time shopper. It will probably require that you work with a large number of mystery shopping companies—perhaps 50, 80 or more. You will have to juggle lots of assignments with different requirements, due dates and report formats, so you must be very organized and disciplined.

Fees for a mystery shop (including purchase reimbursement) may range from about $10 or $20 on up to $50, $100 or more. Fees will depend on the time required, difficulty, etc. The time required to complete a shop and fill out the form may be a few minutes to an hour or longer.

What are the requirements to be a mystery shopper?

You can be any (adult) age, male or female. You may be employed, self-employed, unemployed, retired or a full time homemaker. You need to be observant and able to follow directions. You must be reliable. You don't have to have a degree or any special training or experience, although experience in customer service (such as having worked in hospitality or retail) is helpful. The mystery shopping companies will provide any training you need.

Companies often use the Internet to recruit shoppers, make assignments, and complete reports. Internet access is becoming a necessity to work with most mystery shopping companies, but there are still some which don't require it—especially some of the small, local companies.

How do I apply to be a mystery shopper?

In most cases, you won't be hired directly by the business you're mystery shopping. You'll be hired by a mystery shopping company contracted by the business.

Many mystery shopping companies now have applications at their web sites. That is a fast, easy and free way to apply, because you don't have to print resumes or cover letters, or pay postage. If you find a company that doesn't have an online application, the best way to apply is to send a one-page resume, a one-page letter of interest, and a self-addressed stamped envelope. DON'T CALL unless the company has said that it is OK to do so. Many of these companies have small staffs and they are dealing with hundreds or thousands of shoppers and assignments at a time. They don't have time to chat.

Are there jobs available in my area?

If you live in or regularly travel to an area where there are national or regional chain stores, banks, and restaurants there are certainly mystery shops being done there. Almost any business that does business with the public may be mystery shopped, although most "Mom and Pop"-type businesses don't use mystery shoppers.

New shoppers are being hired all the time as businesses begin new mystery shopping programs, programs are expanded, new locations open, shoppers move or quit, etc. Chances are that there are mystery shopping companies actively seeking mystery shoppers in your area.

Jobs don't exist only in heavily populated areas. There may be more jobs in a major city, but there are also more shoppers competing for those jobs. In fact, you may find yourself in demand if you live in a sparsely populated area because it is often difficult to find shoppers in those areas. Do a good job, and you will be highly valued by mystery shopping companies and schedulers, who will give you as much work as they can.

The mystery shopping companies listed in this book aren't in my hometown. How can I find companies near me?

Most of the mystery shopping companies you will work for will not be located near you, even though they will hire you for jobs in your town.

Many companies (such as those in this book) hire shoppers all over the country or even all over the world. For example, if a mystery shopping company is hired to shop all the locations of a national restaurant chain, they will need shoppers in every town that has one of those restaurants, including your town. But there are also local companies which shop only in your area. To find them, look in your Yellow Pages under "Shopping Services - Commercial" or similar headings.

Is the market saturated, or are there opportunities for new shoppers?

There is a lot of competition for mystery shopping jobs, but there are still opportunities for new shoppers. Mystery shopping companies must constantly recruit because businesses begin new mystery shopping programs, companies get new clients, current mystery shoppers quit or move to a different area, etc.

Additionally, most shops must be rotated among shoppers. For example, if a restaurant is shopped twice a month, and the client requires that a shopper may repeat the shop not more than once every three months, the mystery shopping company will need at least six shoppers (and probably more) just to handle that one location.

What do companies look for when they hire shoppers?

They want to know that you are reliable, observant and able to follow directions. You can demonstrate this by filling out the application accurately and completely. Shoppers need to be able to write comments and narratives, so they want to know that you can produce clear writing with correct grammar and spelling. Many will ask for a writing sample during the application process.

Timeliness is important, so if a company contacts you respond promptly. For example, if you receive an application or contract to complete, return it within days, not weeks. If they contact you about an assignment, respond immediately.

Make it easy for mystery shopping companies to reach you by giving them more than one phone number (e.g., your home and office, a cell phone number).

Let them know what computer software (e.g., Microsoft Word, Excel, etc.) you can use, and if you have Internet access at home or at work. Give them your e-mail address. If you have a fax machine, that's a plus.

Tell them when you are available. Can you only shop evenings and weekends or are you available anytime? Let them know how far you are willing to travel to do a shop. Most of the time they won't pay mileage, so let them know where (and how far) you are willing to go.

Give personal information. Are you married? Do you have kids? Grandkids? Pets? Do you wear glasses? What are your hobbies and interests? Do you own a car? Where do you like to shop? This is not the kind of information you would normally give on a job application, but it can help match you with jobs and get you more assignments.

How long will it take to get my first job?

If you apply to several companies, you may get your first job within three to six weeks. Some shoppers have reported getting their first assignments the very same day they applied, but this isn't typical.

The more companies you apply to, the greater the number of jobs you are eligible for and the sooner you will get an assignment. The more flexible and available you are, the more jobs you can get.

Most of the time, you won't hear from a company unless they have a job for you. So don't worry if you don't hear from some companies right away, or ever. It's probably not personal. They just don't have a need for shoppers in your area. You might consider reapplying in six months or a year.

Is it ethical to work for more than one company?

Most companies understand that you will work for other companies. They know that they can't keep you busy all the time, and you want to work. Whatever you do, though, don't share information about one company with another, and don't share one company's report forms, completed evaluations, or other confidential information with another. Be professional and be discreet.

What will I do when I'm mystery shopping?

You'll be given specific instructions for completing your mystery shop, and the company will provide training (usually in writing or over the phone). They will gladly answer your questions, so don't be afraid to ask. They want you to be comfortable doing the shop, and they want you to get it right.

While you are mystery shopping the business, you will be observing things about cleanliness, service, quality and other standards important to the business and its customers.

Questions on the evaluation might include things like: Were you greeted within 60 seconds? Were the floors clean? Did the person who took your order suggest additional items? Was the salesperson able to demonstrate product knowledge by answering your questions? Was your food fresh and served as you ordered it? Did the cashier count back your change and say thank you? Was the rest room clean and fully stocked with soap and tissue? When you leave the business, you will enter the answers on a report form or write a narrative report describing what you saw.

May I take my spouse, friend or child with me?

Sometimes, if it is a place they would normally go with you. For example, you might take your children to the grocery store or a family restaurant, but perhaps not a more formal restaurant. Don't take anyone else along if they will distract you from properly completing your assignment, or if you have not been told that you may.

Remember you are a *mystery* shopper. If you have young children, don't tell them you're mystery shopping. You don't want them asking, loudly, in the middle of a shop, "Mommy, are we doing the mystery shop now?" Adults who accompany you must know that they are not to talk about mystery shopping or give away that you are the shopper.

Will the employees know that I'm the mystery shopper?

No. At first, you might feel like you have a neon sign that says MYSTERY SHOPPER blinking on your forehead, but they really won't know. If for some reason someone asks you if you are the mystery shopper, just say no or play dumb. "Mystery shopper? What's that?"

Will I be asked to do anything odd or to be "difficult"?

I've had to ask questions I thought were kind of silly, and I had to try to buy a pair of mismatched shoes (to see if the cashier caught it). But I've never been asked to make a scene, try to trick someone, be obnoxious, attempt to steal, or anything else that I wouldn't want to do. Each job will be explained to you. If you are at all uncomfortable with it, turn it down.

If I turn down a job, will they offer jobs in the future?

Probably. I've turned down jobs because they were too far away, they weren't right for me, or I just didn't have time. Those companies called me later with other jobs. Of course, it's a little like dating: If you say no every time they call, they will eventually stop calling.

This sounds great! How do I get started?

Follow the Action Plan on page 121. Write your resume and letter of interest, and start applying to companies. Don't forget to contact the local companies you find in the Yellow Pages. While I can't guarantee that you will get a certain number of assignments, if you follow the instructions here you will get hired. The more companies you apply to, the more jobs you can get.

About the Author

Cathy Stucker has been mystery shopping since 1995, and she has helped thousands of people learn how to get paid to shop and eat through her seminars and her book, *The Mystery Shopper's Manual.*

When she's not shopping, Cathy Stucker is The Idea Lady™. She helps entrepreneurs, professionals, authors and publishers attract customers and make themselves famous with inexpensive, creative and fun marketing techniques.

Cathy provides hands-on help through her consulting services, and teaches clients as well as do-it-yourselfers in seminars and teleclasses. She also publishes manuals, special reports, booklets, audio tapes and ebooks with step-by-step instructions anyone can use successfully.

Cathy Stucker has instructed courses for a number of colleges and universities, including the University of Houston, Houston Community College, Collin County Community College, Lee College, et al. She is a former seminar leader for Fred Pryor Seminars, and regularly presents seminars for many continuing education programs, community and business organizations.

Cathy is a frequent media guest. In addition to many appearances on Houston-area television programs, she has been a guest on radio programs from coast to coast. Cathy has been featured in *The Houston Chronicle, The Houston Business Journal, Black Enterprise, Woman's Day* and many others.

When she is not being written about, Cathy is writing. She is a prolific author whose articles have been published in national magazines and other print and electronic publications. She has created a variety of information products, and she is a member of the board of the Association of Authors and Publishers <http://www.authorsandpublishers.org/>. One of Cathy's publications is in the collection of the George H. W. Bush Presidential Library.

For more information about Cathy Stucker, visit her on the web at http://www.IdeaLady.com. To request a free subscription to her weekly ezine, *Bright Ideas!*, visit http://www.IdeaLady.com/bright.htm. Newsletter editors, ezine editors and webmasters will find articles that may be reprinted free of charge at http://www.IdeaLady.com/content.htm.

To schedule a consultation or media interview, call Cathy at 281-265-7342. She may be reached via email at cathy@idealady.com.

Want to order
The Mystery Shopper's Manual
for your friends?

Use the handy order form
on the next page!

Orders may be faxed, phoned, mailed or emailed. Or you may order online at http://www.IdeaLady.com/.

Fax: 281-265-9727

Phone: 888-266-5888 (toll-free)

Email: orders@idealady.com

Postal Mail: Special Interests Publishing, 4646 Hwy 6, #123, Sugar Land, TX 77478

Be sure to see all the
great resources available at
IdeaLady.com!

While you're there,
sign up for our free email newsletters!

ORDER FORM
Special Interests Publishing
4646 Hwy 6,#123
Sugar Land, Texas 77478
281-265-7342 / 1-888-266-5888

**View the Special Interests Catalog online at
www.IdeaLady.com**

I would like to order the following items:

_____

_____

_____

Add $5 shipping (per order, not per item) in the
U.S., $12 for International orders.
Texas residents, add 8.25% sales tax.

For credit card (Visa/Master Card/Discover) orders:

Card Number: _____

Exp. Date: _____ Signature: _____

Name: _____

Address: _____

City/State/Zip: _____

Phone: _____

Email: _____

____ Check here to receive our free email newsletter.
(Be sure to include your email address.)